"10 TO WIN"

THE TOP TEN WAYS TO WIN IN LIFE & BUSINESS

STEVE WILMER

Copyright © 2016 by Steve Speaks LLC

All rights reserved.

No part of this publication may be reproduced, distributed, or transmitted in any form or by any means, including photocopying, recording, or other electronic or mechanical methods, without the prior written permission of the publisher, except in the case of brief quotations embodied in critical reviews and certain other noncommercial uses permitted by copyright law. For permission requests, write to the publisher, addressed "Attention: Permissions Coordinator," at the address below.

Apex Media & Publishing LLC
6847 N. 9th Ave Ste A #336
Pensacola, Fl 32504
www.ApexMediaPublishing.com

Ordering Information:
Quantity sales. Special discounts are available on quantity purchases by corporations, associations, and others. For details, contact the publisher at the address above.

ISBN-13: 978-0692660812 (Paperback)
ISBN-10: 0692660812X

Published by Apex Media & Publishing LLC
Written by Stephen C. Wilmer
Edited by Ervin Byrd
Cover & Interior Design by Elden Scott

Published in the United States of America

Contents

ACKNOWLEDGEMENTS
DEDICATION
INTRODUCTION
CHAPTER ONE
    SCREAM THE DREAM 1
CHAPTER TWO
    I'M NOT HUNGRY 21
CHAPTER THREE
    PUSH OR PULL 37
CHAPTER FOUR
    PUMP YOUR BRAKES 53
CHAPTER FIVE
    ALL OUT 63
CHAPTER SIX
    FIND A NEW ROOM 81
CHAPTER SEVEN
    NO ONE IS WATCHING 95
CHAPTER EIGHT
    GOLD VS. PLATINUM 107
CHAPTER NINE
    JUMP 123
CHAPTER TEN
    THE MAIN THING 135
CONCLUSION

ACKNOWLEDGEMENTS

A very special thank you to my family for their understanding, patience and continued support of my dreams. I am blessed with four loving children who admire their dad and are quick to forgive when I make mistake after mistake. Judah, Josiah, Joi, and Jayna, I love you. I am equally blessed with a wife who from day one has stood beside me every time I wanted to "Jump" into a new venture. There is no doubt in my mind that had it not been for you, I would not be where I am today. You are my biggest cheerleader. I love you with all my heart Erin Wilmer. 143

I would like to acknowledge five men who served as father figures to me throughout the years: My great uncle, retired Army Staff Sergeant Charles Packer, my Marine Corps Sergeant Kenny Green, my Police Field Training Officer David Alexander III, my former Pastor in Waukegan Illinois, Apostle Leon C. Cosey Jr., and my current Pastor Anthony McMillan. These men will never truly understand how much they have impacted my life. Thank you, gentlemen, for being that father figure that every man needs and inwardly desires. I am a better man because of the time that each of you invested in my life.

I have had many supporters along my journey, and I appreciate their support; however, I would like to specifically recognize several individuals who saw something in me, told me that my dreams were possible and encouraged me to pursue them. Thank you for constantly speaking success over my life. Francis Peters, Darlene Wynder, David Anderson, Mary Riesberg, John Kizziah, Eddie Hill, Willie Spears, Rob Hazewinkel & Bill Whitley; may God bless each of you with a double portion of the blessings you have spoken into my life.

A special thank you to Elden Scott, who lead the way in helping make one of my dreams to become a published author a reality. You went "All Out" on this book and pushed me to get it done. You are the reason that my message is being shared today rather than five years from today. Thank you for your work on this my friend.

Dedication

This book is dedicated to those individuals who have had a less than easy life growing up. You had to fight for everything you've ever gotten. Not because your parent(s) didn't love you, but because they didn't have it to give. I am living proof that dreams do come true, often accompanied by blood, sweat and tears. May you be blessed and encouraged by the words in this book.

"If you believe in yourself and have dedication and pride and never quit, you'll be a winner. The price of victory is high, but so are the rewards."
-Paul "Bear" Bryant

INTRODUCTION

There are many keys to one's success. It's also important to recognize that success is not a destination, but rather a journey. Every individual should determine what success means to him or her. Do not allow others (society) to make that determination for you, less you will never live up to their standards. This is your journey and you are in control of which paths you take. I wanted to share with you my journey, and I hope in doing so it will help you, inspire you, and caution you against some of the mistakes that I have made.

Wanting to write the best book that I possibly could, I was told by many people to make sure that I had a good editor. It's important to make sure that the stories flow in order, there is no redundancy, no dangling participles (not sure what those are) and of course, there are no grammatical errors. My editors were excellent. They caught many errors, suggested many changes, and the words they recommended were exquisite… but they were not my words. I wanted you to hear directly from me. No filter. This is who I am, unpolished and straight forward. I hope that you will focus on the message, rather than sentence structure. Enjoy!

From the projects...to my passion, who would have "thunk" it?

I was born in Pensacola, Florida to a single mother, Norma Jean on welfare. No father in the home, no father in my life for that matter. We moved from place to place, including the Aragon Court projects, before finally having to move in with my grandmother during my high school years. I still remember standing in the welfare lines to receive food, or often times having to take a bath at a friend's house because our utilities had been shut off for non-payment. It wasn't until I was older that I realized that it was not normal to have roaches and rats as pets. Like most poor single women with children, I'm sure my mother did the best she could. I was never hungry, always had clothes to wear, and being an only child allowed for a few more toys at Christmas.

Norma Jean succeeded in keeping me out of trouble as a youth, unlike most of my childhood friends. She never had much to give me, but deep down I knew that she loved me; although, she may not have expressed it as much as I desired. She had a short life, dying unexpectedly at the age of sixty-one. Before her death, I remember praying with my mother as she accepted Christ as her Savior. I preached her eulogy in 2002. I miss her dearly.

I was a below average student in the public schools of

Escambia County, always seeming to barely get by. I wasn't the class clown but I did attempt to use humor to hide the fact that I really did have a difficult time learning things. I specifically remember one of my high school teachers telling me in front of the class that I would never amount to anything. The laughs and the "oohs" from the other students are still clear as a bell today. Of course she turned out to be wrong, but as a child I believed her.

After barely graduating high school (GPA 1.9), I enlisted in the United States Marine Corps. Once I excelled as a Marine Corps Infantryman, I knew that I could accomplish anything that I wanted. I did a lot of growing up in those four years. If I had to choose one thing that set me on the right path it would have to be my time in the Corps. It was over 30 years ago and I am still part of a brotherhood that will live forever. Semper Fi. I then spent the next 10 years serving my community with three different law enforcement agencies from Florida to Illinois. At times, I found myself on the opposite side of the law from some of my childhood friends from the projects.

After meeting and marrying my wife Erin, we decided to start a family and that meant a more stable schedule. I traded my badge and gun (well…the badge anyway) for a bag of mail at the US Post Office. Although it was a fairly simple job with great pay, I knew right away that I could not spend the next

30 years delivering paper from house-to-house. I knew that I had to do something different, but I just didn't know what that would be until a friend of mine invited me to a meeting that would change the course of my life. You will read all about it in Chapter 2. My next leap of faith came when I began a successful insurance career. My success in that career launched my business as a speaker, trainer, and now, author.

The 10 concepts that I share with you in "10 To Win" are the life lessons that I have learned and continue to grow in, by implementing them in my life every day. These are solid biblical based concepts, backed by scripture that will have a positive effect on your life when utilized. Notice I said "utilized", because you must use them in order to make a change. In this book I share my personal and very private experiences that I have been through. I hope that my successes and failures will be a blessing to every reader's life. My desire is that as you read this book, you are able to evaluate your life and make a definite change to reach your life goals.

"10 TO WIN"

THE TOP TEN WAYS TO WIN IN LIFE & BUSINESS

CHAPTER 1

SCREAM THE DREAM

"10 To Win"

My staff is getting the last minute details taken care of. They are making sure that everything is in place, and everyone knows what their responsibilities are. They know how I like things done, and they want to make sure there are no hiccups along the way. They have been coordinating with the Civic Center all month long and today the event is finally here. They have done an outstanding job, and I am proud of their work. They always make me look good. Over 10,000 tickets have been sold, and the place will be packed. I have been receiving congratulations and well wishes from friends and family all month long. They have been anxiously awaiting to attend the event as well.

Of course, I am a little nervous, but I try to eat a good breakfast because Erin is not letting me out of the house without putting something in my stomach. She always takes good care of me. I thank God for my wife. She is my leading supporter. The kids are quiet this morning and not fussing with each other, as usual. I know that Erin has given them "the talk." We all gather in a circle and pray before we leave home. It's Friday, and it's my turn to pray (Friday-Father prays). I finish, and I ask my oldest son, Judah, to say a special prayer for me. Sometimes I can be so hard on him because he is the oldest. I let him know how much I love him, appreciate him and how extremely proud of him I am. He finishes praying, and I say thank you as I give him a big hug. He smiles from ear to ear because all he wants is for his dad to be proud of him, and let him know it.

Fathers, make sure that your children know how much you love them and how you are proud of them. We can't afford to lose our children to these streets. We are living in some challenging times regarding the upbringing of our kids. They need to feel our love on a daily basis. They may not get it right all the time. They may make mistakes from time to time, even huge mistakes. But they should never doubt the fact that we love them. Ever! We mess up all the time as well, but our Heavenly Father still loves us without conditions. He may not like some of the things we think, say or do, but it doesn't change His love for us. Romans 8:38-39 says, *"For I am convinced that neither death nor life, neither angels or demons, neither the present nor the future, nor any powers, neither height nor depth, nor anything else in all creation, will be able to separate us from the love of God that is in Christ Jesus our Lord.*" God should be our example when it comes to raising the children He blessed and entrusted to us.

As we load up in the van for our drive to the Pensacola Civic Center, my daughter Jayna (6) is singing, Joi (8) has her headphones on and is watching a movie on the DVD player, as Judah (14) and Josiah (12) are playing video games in the backseat. Erin is holding my right hand as I drive, smiling at me and making sure that I'm okay. She can tell that I'm nervous. I could not do this without her. Thank God that I don't have to. We arrive and meet my staff. They inform me that everything is a "go", and there are no issues. They are full of smiles, everyone in uniform (khaki pants/white polo shirt with "Steve Speaks" logo). I have on my favorite dark blue suit, white shirt with red "power" tie, brown belt and brown shoes to match with my signature blue & brown Oxford socks. Of course, I am wearing my American flag lapel pin. For all of our flaws, I love my country. As Erin and the kids get ready to head to their seats, my youngest Jayna gives me a big hug and so does my son Josiah. They are both huggers. Growing up, I didn't give or receive many hugs. Jayna and Josiah have changed that.

Men, there is nothing like giving a hug to your son and telling him that you love him. I used to think that it wasn't the manly thing to do. Sometimes that's what the world tells us.

Don't listen. Show affection for those whom you love, especially your children and especially your sons. I show my sons love so that they don't receive the wrong type of "love" from the gang bangers in the streets. I show my daughters love so that they don't receive the wrong type of "love" from men in the streets. It's our responsibility as fathers to validate our daughters. We are examples of what they will look for in a husband.

My family takes their seats as my staff and I hold hands and say a quick prayer. They put on my lapel microphone and give it a quick test as I can hear someone on stage introducing me. They are reading my bio, and I still cannot believe that I am here. I am nervous and fearful as I always am before I speak, so that's a good sign. I take a deep breath, say another short prayer to myself as I always do before any program, "Father God, I thank you for today. I pray Lord God that the words I speak today will be your words and not mine. I decrease that you may increase. I pray that people's lives will be changed and you will receive all the glory. In Jesus' name I pray. Amen." I hear my name called, and I walk out on stage. The Civic Center is packed, and everyone is applauding…loudly. As the audience quiets down, I begin to speak. The nervousness goes away, and God begins to move. The title of my speech is, "I'm not supposed to be here."

I speak passionately from my heart about my upbringing, life lessons, failures and success. I can see that people are touched. Erin always says, "What's from the heart touches the heart." I share my life story with the audience through facts, testimonies, stories and humor. There is something that everyone can relate to. God is moving, and at times, I am even brought to tears.

I know that my buddy Joel Dunham will jokingly make fun of me because a tough Marine is not supposed to cry. Again, don't believe it, men. It's okay to cry, especially in front of your sons. They need to know that real men aren't afraid to show emotion. Real men cry…when it's appropriate. I had a drill instructor once tell me that every time I hear the National Anthem or The Marine's Hymn, it should bring a tear to my eye. And to this day, it still does.

I finish speaking, and I receive a standing ovation. I know for a fact that lives have been touched and changed this day. Thank you, Lord. As I leave the stage, there is a line of people to shake my hand and thank me for today. What I had to say (what God had to say through me) was a revelation to them. I can see my team off in the distance at the table selling my books. Jayna cuts in line to give me a big hug and tell me that she loves me. I pause from shaking hands with people to acknowledge my family and receive hugs and kisses from them.

"10 To Win"

Let's remember to always take a minute, or however long it takes to acknowledge our family. Allow them to "cut line" and make sure they always come first. They are our strength. I have to make sure that I remember this lesson from time to time, myself. I thank you, God, for my family.

Erin leaves with the kids as I will be here for a while shaking hands, taking pictures (selfies) and autographing books. Someone from my team will give me a ride later. After all the hands have been shaken and books signed, we leave for home.

As I sit in the passenger seat, exhausted because I gave everything I had, I think about the road it took to get here. All the patience, the sacrifices, the hard work, dedication & determination has paid off. I am living my dream as a speaker and author. Who would have thought, a little black boy from the projects of Pensacola was the man on that stage. I am truly blessed and humbled. As I drift off to sleep while being driven home, I am reminded that all this started with a dream that I had. It's a dream that I screamed to anyone that would listen, a dream that I would put in my first book, and a dream that you are reading at this very moment.

That is my dream folks: To speak before a large crowd at the Pensacola Civic Center. It was vivid, right down to the last detail including the color of my socks. Some of you may have thought that this event actually took place. I believe that one day it will. I don't know how I'm going to get there. But I'm going to do all that I can to make sure that I do get there. If I should fail, it won't be because I didn't do the work. It won't be because I didn't take action. I have a plan in place, and I am following that plan on a daily basis. Sometimes I may have to tweak the plan or form a new plan, but there is always a plan, and I am always working my plan.

When you started your business, you had a business plan. Well, I sincerely hope that you had a business plan. If not, I suggest that you write one. A business plan is like a road map to success. It lays out exactly what you will need to do in order for you to succeed. It has everything in it: the cost of goods, business location, market analysis, pitfalls, remedies, ups, downs, pros, cons, everything. It is impossible to succeed in business without a plan in place. You cannot simply wing it or shoot from the hip. You have to put certain measures in place to enhance your chances of success.

When I was applying for an insurance agency, I had to write a business plan. It was overwhelming at first, and I didn't want to do it. But I knew it would improve my chances for success, so I wrote my plan. Again, simply writing the plan is not enough, we have to be disciplined and follow our plan to achieve that success.

Habakkuk 2:2 says, *"Write the vision, and make it plain upon tables, that he may run that readeth it."* A vision is like a dream. Write your dream down. Use it as a blueprint for your business and your life. Follow it, run with it and make changes when necessary. Sometimes we may have to fire employees who do not have the same vision as we do. We may also have to fire friends and relatives who do not have the same vision as we do. We have to let go of what's killing us, even when it's killing us to let go.

Rob's Dream - About ten years ago, I had the opportunity to meet Russ, the franchise owner of MaxFit Sports Nutrition. I learned about his stores, the franchise, and what it takes to become an owner. The more we talked, the more I fell in love with this business model and store. Having been involved in sports & wrestling, this was right up my alley! My dream started to form. I started reading books and talking to Russ as much as I could. I began to visualize owning my own store. After being turned down by the bank numerous times, I made the decision to sell my other business and go all out. Two months later, I was able to purchase a MaxFit Sports Nutrition store (located in Pace, FL).
- Rob Hazewinkel

Business owners have a business plan to help run their business. But how many of us have a business plan for our family? How many of us have taken the time to sit down and write out a plan to make sure our marriage will be a success? Isn't our family just as important if not more important than business? I have been married for 18 years, and initially, I tried to wing it. I tried to shoot from the hip. Every married man can tell you that doesn't work.

You have to be deliberate about the success of your marriage, the relationship with your children and anything else that you wish to achieve. No one graduates from college by winging it. You have to be deliberate about your studies. You must have a plan, a blueprint for success. The enemy, the tempter, the devil, satan, whatever you want to call him always has a plan to destroy marriages. And he is working his plan diligently. 1Peter 5:8 says, *"Be alert and of sober mind. Your enemy the devil prowls around like a roaring lion looking for someone to devour."* I've heard that the divorce rate today is approximately 50%. Unfortunately, it's no surprise when we hear that someone got divorced or no surprise when we hear that a business closed or shut down. So if you want your marriage or business to succeed, then follow a blueprint. Follow a plan, and be diligent about it.

Dream and imagine what you want your family and/or business to look like. Imagine it the way that I imagined my speaking at the civic center. See every little detail about your spouse, your children, your job, your business, your event, whatever it is that you want to achieve. Then write it down. Share it with others, especially with those who genuinely want to see you succeed. Stay away from dream stealers and dream killers. The best blueprint I've seen for marriage is the Bible. It has great advice for husbands and wives and men and women in general. There are lots of other blueprints to use as workbooks as well. The Five Love Languages by Gary Chapman was a great blueprint for my wife and I. More on this in Chapter 8.

Rodney's Dream - *For so many years, I have had dreams and have let them be smothered by "the now". I had the mentality that "the now" was so important, and the future was just wishing. My dream is to own a coffee shop where I would serve my very own baked goods. My coffee shop would be unique (can't share the details here). I would also like to be an active liaison for a non-profit organization whose sole purpose is to minister in every way to those who are destitute in every way. - Rodney Stovall*

You see, the problem with dreams is reality. You can dream about your business, your family, that job, those finances, etc. But the reality is that if you don't take action, your dreams will never happen. Everyone has a dream, yes, including you. But sadly, most people have given up on their dreams. They have accepted the status quo. I know this because I was there. I was one of those people. I allowed fear to stop me from pursuing my dream for years. Wait until you get to Chapter 9. You will discover once and for all how to put fear behind you and never allow it to stop you again.

David's Dream - *I was a dreamer from early childhood. It was pretty clear that I've always dreamed of being a good person and making a positive difference in the community. When I applied for the job of my dream, police officer, I was asked during my interview, "Where do you see yourself in five years?" My response was that I would be "a Lieutenant, a Captain, or even the Chief of Police." My ambition was apparent in my answer, but my dream was the driving force for my ambition. For many years following, I've reflected on that answer, on that dream, and I have even questioned what others may have thought of my answer. I'm grateful that over the years, I was able to embrace the validity of that dream and pursue it. I am now the Chief of Police for the Pensacola Police Department. I'm living my dream.*
- Chief David Alexander III

I mentioned earlier that we have to stay away from dream stealers and dream killers. These people don't want us to pursue our dream because they have either given up on their dream and want to crush ours, or they simply don't believe it's possible for us to achieve it. It doesn't matter the reason, stay away from them and don't listen to them. An old Chinese proverb reads, "The person who says that it can't be done should not interrupt the person doing it." Unfortunately, sometimes these people are our friends and family. They love us, and they mean well, but they have simply given up on their dreams. They say things like, "Be realistic, it's too late, you're too old, you're too young, you're not smart enough, there's not enough money, not enough time, and it's impossible." They never have an encouraging word.

Sometimes this negative person is "us". We say to ourselves that it can't be done. Just like a dream starts in your mind, so does doubt. Whichever you give your focus to will grow: Your doubts vs. your dreams. So, start giving life to your dreams, and stop that negative thinking about your qualifications or lack thereof. Start or grow that business, strengthen your marriage, your relationship, etc. You already have what it takes inside of you to be successful. God put it there. It's up to you to use it.

Lance's Dream - *I believe in our church's (True Worship Assembly of God) mission to reach the community and the world* *with the Gospel of Jesus Christ. And so, I believe I have the capacity and opportunities in life to achieve my dream of funding our church's expansion as well as the missionaries we support. Secondly, I have a dream to take the company my grandfather founded, Rubber & Specialties, Inc., to a global market. Typically, we only compete locally with each brand, but I believe we can go far beyond our state lines.   - Lance Cook*

You have to see it before you see it. Let me put it another way. You have to dream it before it can become a reality. Pastor and author, Anthony McMillan says, "Visualize your dream (see it), vocalize your dream (speak it) and vitalize your dream (work it)." This is such an important message that it's the quote I use on my business card. "The distance between your dreams and reality is called... ACTION!!!"

I never liked math while I was growing up, and I wasn't very good at it either. Actually, 4 out of 3 people have trouble with math. So this may seem strange coming from me, but here is a math formula for success in whatever area that you wish to succeed. DREAM + ACTION = REALITY. Of course, there will be some subtraction as well. Subtract DOUBT, FEAR and NEGATIVE PEOPLE from the equation. After you subtract, then remember to carry the "1" forward, that is, FOCUS. That which you consistently think about and focus on most always becomes your maximum potential. So change your focus and you will change your potential. See it before you see it also means having faith. Faith is that personal conviction that what you wish to achieve in life and business will come to pass, regardless of what the situation currently looks like.

Hebrews 11:1 says, *"Now faith is having confidence in what we hope for although we do not see it."* I know that it may be difficult, but we can't be moved by our circumstances. Our circumstances only determine where we currently are, not where we are going. Also, remember that we are not a product of our circumstances, but rather a product of our decisions. So let's start making wise decisions, shall we?

Aerialle's Dream - *Growing up, I always knew I wanted to be my own boss. I knew I had a dream; and with that, I could formulate a plan. I have always taken interests in the latest fashion. I am currently a business major in college pursuing my degree. My dream is to open my own business selling fashionable men's wear. I have created a plan, set goals, and began acting towards my lifelong desire. With hard work and dedication, I know that success will come. I am eager to finish what I have started.*
- Aerialle Bradley 19

Author and speaker, Bill Whitley always says that ideas alone are not valuable. It's only when you implement the idea that they become truly valuable. It's also been said that the graveyard is full of people who had potential. Don't let your ideas and your dreams die inside of you or die with you. Act on them; pursue them with all your focus. Make those dreams become a reality. Don't waste year after year like I did. Avoid these: doubting yourself, negative self-talk, thinking you are less than what it takes to get there. Those are all lies. Implement those ideas, talents and gifts that God has given you. I am now traveling around the country teaching, training and motivating individuals to achieve their goals. I am living my dream. So can you.

Darlene's Dream - My belief, that children are our future, is the inspiration for my dream. My dream is to own and operate an Early Childhood Learning Center (not your average day-care). My desire is to impact our future leaders at an early age while their minds are most impressionable. Not only will this be my business, but a family endeavor as well. We are blessed to have several family members with a heart for education. - Darlene Wynder

Surround yourself with those individuals who make your baby leap. Luke 1:41 says, *"When Elizabeth heard Mary's greeting, the baby leaped in her womb."* Surround yourself with those individuals who make your baby (your dream) leap. They always have positive things to say to you regarding your baby (your dream). They encourage you, support you and sometimes challenge you. But it's always with love to make sure that you're growing and going in the right direction. Do you make babies leap when you open your mouth? Or are you Negative Nelly or Realistic Randy? I apologize if your name is Nelly or Randy. Don't be like these two.

In the movie, <u>The Pursuit of Happyness</u>, Will Smith plays the role of Chris Gardner, a father struggling to care for himself and his 6-year old son, with little or no financial means. In one scene the son is playing basketball and says to his dad, "I'm going pro." Immediately, the dad begins to tell his son not to get his hopes up and that he would probably just be below average because he himself was below average. The son agrees and then throws the basketball to the ground in disappointment. Seeing his son's reaction, the dad then changes his words to his son. He says, "Don't ever let somebody tell you that you can't do something, not even me. You got a dream? You gotta protect it! When people can't do something themselves, they want to tell you that you can't do it. If you want something, go get it. Period!"

***Dia's Dream** - Three years ago my dream was to create the world's first socially responsible dating site for those wishing to avoid sexually transmitted diseases. SwaggerScan.com was created to offer a safer alternative to online dating and to give people*

a reason to get tested. I've created what medical professionals have confirmed as "a powerful online tool" for those who are aware of their own status to communicate with others of similar values. I encourage you to pursue your dreams and hope you are compelled to help me follow mine. - Dia Hicks

Parents, what are we saying to our children? Are we encouraging them to shoot for the stars? Or, are we transferring our negative attitudes and shortcomings to them? I wasn't able to do it, so you won't be able either? Or is it the complete opposite? You didn't follow your dreams, so now you're making your children do what you didn't do. It's your dream, not theirs. Do what Chris Gardner did. He quickly changed his words to his son and encouraged him. He made his son's "baby" leap. It's never too late to change what we think, say and do. You should be quick to apologize to your children, and admit it whenever you are wrong and ask for forgiveness. They will forgive you. They just want to be loved by you and want you to be proud of them. It's simple. Don't make it more difficult than it is. Who makes your baby leap? Who always supports you and encourages you? That's who you talk to. That's who you listen to.

This chapter is called "Scream the Dream" because it's meant for you to tell your dream to those around you. First, when you speak your dream, it gives your dream life.

Proverbs 18:21 says, *"The power of life and death is in the tongue and those that love it will eat its fruit."* Joel Osteen talks about the power of "I Am". Basically, whatever you say will come to pass. If you say that you have a successful business and start working towards it, then that's what you shall have. By the same token, if you say that your business is struggling (regardless if it's currently true) then that's what you will have. Joel says, "Whatever you say will come looking for you."

"Lord I thank you that my business is prosperous, that my marriage is fulfilling, and that my children are healthy."

When you scream your dream, you are speaking life into your dream, and you shall reap the benefits (fruit) of your dream. When I started saying that I would be a top insurance producer and began working towards it, it happened. When I started saying that I would become a professional speaker and began to get my presentations together, the call came, and now I'm doing it. When I started saying that my marriage would be blessed and started working towards it, it became blessed. Whatever your dream may be, start speaking it. Start seeing it before you see it. Have faith.

Romans 4:17 talks about, *"...calling those things that be*

not as though they were." Don't be moved by what you see in the natural. Be moved by what God says about you and your dream. Scream it to the top of your lungs if you have to. Right now, stop and think about your dream. It doesn't matter if it's a new dream or an old dream that you forgot somewhere along the line in your journey of life. Say it aloud. Don't worry if it sounds silly, just try it. Say your dream aloud. Say what it is that you want God to do in your life and your business. Say it and keep saying it over and over. Tell someone (the right person) what it is. Start working towards it, have faith and watch God move on your behalf. "Scream the Dream".

#1 IN ORDER TO WIN IN LIFE &BUSINESS, YOU HAVE TO DREAM. THEN YOU HAVE TO PUT A PLAN IN PLACE AND TAKE ACTION TO MAKE SURE THAT DREAM COMES FULL CIRCLE. YOU SHALL HAVE WHAT YOU SAY.

"If your dreams don't scare you, then they're not big enough." - Ellen Sirleaf

"If you don't build your dream, someone will hire you to help build theirs." - Tony Gaskins

Notes:

CHAPTER 2

I'M NOT HUNGRY

"10 To Win"

After high school I enlisted in the United States Marine Corps. After four years of active duty and four years reserves, I was honorably discharged at the start of Desert Storm (I served in Desert Shield). I then had a ten year law enforcement career before moving on to the United States Post Office as a Letter Carrier and Supervisor. I'd never sold anything a day in my life. One evening, a post office co-worker, invited me to a meeting after work. When I inquired about what type of meeting it was, he was hesitant to say. Since I trusted him, I decided to go along for the ride.

When we arrived at the hotel, he walked me to the banquet room. I could hear loud upbeat music playing in the distance. As we entered the room, it was packed with a diverse group of people. Everyone had smiles on their faces and were very quick to introduce themselves to me and thank me for coming. There were others in the room who had that "deer in the headlights" look just as I did. Apparently, they were brought there as well without knowing why. After fifteen minutes or so, the music stopped and a gentleman walked to the front of the room. He thanked everyone for coming, spoke for a few minutes and began to introduce someone else. As he did so, the entire room erupted in applause and stood on their feet. A second man began to run to the front of the room. He was a young man in his mid 20's, fairly good looking with dark black hair. I did not recognize his nationality. I would later discover that he was from Albania, which is just north of Greece.

When the crowd finally settled down, he began to speak. His English was broken, a little slow, but very deliberate. As he spoke, the audience was silent. His words and his story drew me in. I found myself hanging on his every word, waiting to see how the story ended. The short version is that he left Albania unable to speak any English, traveled to America to find that American Dream that we all hear about, became a pizza delivery driver, and now was making $100,000 in residual income.

Yep, you guessed it. I was at a network marketing meeting, a get rich quick, pyramid scheme meeting. The funny thing is this, I believed it. It made sense. I could make an extra $1,000 month, without having to quit my job and without having to get a part-time job punching a clock somewhere. I mean, who doesn't want an extra $1,000 a month right? The company was AmeriPlan and they were (still are) offering dental benefits. When the gentleman finished speaking, I just had to meet him. I waited in line and finally was able to speak with this young superstar. His name is Andi Duli. I told him that I enjoyed his presentation and told him my background as well. Remember, I had no sales experience. I went on to say that while I believed that this could be done, I also knew the negative stigma of this type of business. We discussed it briefly. I then told Andi that I would enroll as a representative, but I would not be one of those people who told everybody about it. I would not be bringing friends and family to meetings like this. I would try to sell the benefits, but I wouldn't make it a big deal. Andi looked at me sincerely and said these words that made me a top salesman over the next ten years. He said, "Steve, nothing happens until you get excited."

AmeriPlan "Rising Star" Award - Steve Wilmer

These simple words were about to propel me to new heights. And they will do the same for you. Regardless of what you wish to accomplish, you must get excited first. Now say it aloud to yourself: Nothing happens until I get excited. Say it again - Nothing happens until I get excited. Say it one more time and louder this time. NOTHING HAPPENS UNTIL I GET EXCITED! This is the first step in any goal, endeavor, dream, task or whatever it is that you wish to do.

Now don't get me wrong, the world is full of average people going through their daily lives barely moving and barely getting it done. They do the least that is required of them, just enough to get by. We know these people. They aren't excited about anything. They have no goals or dreams and are completely happy with whatever life gives them. I call these people "clock watchers." You know them. They watch the clock to see when break time will be here. They watch the clock to see how soon lunch will be here. They watch the clock to see how soon 5 p.m. will be here so they can quit working. They live for Friday. Every Sunday night they get a pain in their stomach because they know that tomorrow is Monday, and they have to go back to that job/business that they hate. And unfortunately, we also know someone who feels this way about the personal relationship they're in as well. Normally, these are the people that wait for their ship to come in, rather than swim out to the ship. They wait for the opportunity to knock rather than kicking in the door. You get the point. They are not excited about anything, and yet at times, they still manage to get things done. So maybe I should clarify the term "Get Excited" by saying that, to accomplish Great Things, you have to get excited.

Andi was absolutely right. I became excited about AmeriPlan. Remember, up until this point, I'd never sold anything before. I began talking to everyone about dental benefits. I talked to the people at work, the people on my route, my friends, strangers, EVERYONE. I thought about new ways to spread the word about my business constantly. Everyone who knew me knew about AmeriPlan. The checks were coming in on a weekly basis, customers were receiving much needed dental benefits, I was building a solid team and gaining national recognition. I was now the speaker at the hotel and people came to see me, just as I'd come to see Andi.

My wife Erin was not initially on board with my new business, but when she saw my excitement, and our first paycheck, then she became excited as well. Excitement is contagious. She actually started training our team in our home on a weekly basis. You see, my excitement was able to change her outlook on the situation. Our excitement helped us build a team of over three hundred people, and my team got excited.

AmeriPlan had never heard of Pensacola before, but now large amounts of revenue were flowing in, and AmeriPlan got excited. After working my business part-time for eighteen months, I was able to replace my post office income, and then I really got excited. So after praying to God, and getting permission from my wife, I quit the post office and went into commission sales full time.

Talk about a leap of faith. But I truly believed that God had better things in store for the Wilmer family, and I was having fun at the same time. Incidentally, I believe that the concept of network marketing is brilliant. It gives the average person, like me, the opportunity to become a business owner with a small monetary investment. You receive mentors, referred to as an up-line, who are vested in making sure that you succeed. If you succeed, they make more money. You are able to climb as high as you would like, depending on how hard you are willing to work. Most employees will never be the CEO of the company, no matter how hard they work.

Erin would always have to tell me to stop and eat something. I was so excited and having so much fun, I would simply say, "I'm Not Hungry." Food was the last thing on my mind. I just wanted to keep working. When kids are outside playing and having fun, you literally have to make them stop, come inside and eat. They stuff the food down quickly and are right back to it again. They are having fun doing what they love to do…PLAY. I was having fun doing what I loved to do. Motivational speaker Eric Thomas once said that Beyoncé was in the studio for three days before she realized that she hadn't eaten. Please note that he did not say that Beyoncé purposely skipped her meal. I never purposely skipped my meals either. We were so focused and having so much fun doing what we loved to do, doing what we were created to do, that we simply forgot to eat. The kids forgot to eat. In writing this book, Erin gets upset with me because I won't stop to eat when I sit down and start writing. I'm not hungry! I'm having fun!

Lots of people, including some family members, said that I was crazy for leaving a good job like the post office. They meant well, but they didn't understand that working that job for 30+ years was not my destiny. Ask yourself, "Am I living my destiny? Am I meant to be here?" Now, there is nothing wrong with working a job 'til retirement. It's honorable to give a hard day's work and enjoy what you're doing. There are many benefits to retirement. Erin spent twenty-four years serving her country in the United States Navy and retired. Our family is now reaping the benefits of her dedication. Unfortunately, most people work their job not because they love it, but because they don't believe that they can do anything else. It's the same reason most people stay in a bad relationship. It all boils down to fear and self-doubt. These two things I suffered from for years, and to this day they still try to creep in.

The key is starting to believe what God says about you. Are you a business owner or desire to be a business owner? Deuteronomy 8:18 says, *"For it is He (God) who gives you the ability to produce wealth."* We all have the ability, but most of us aren't using the ability he gave us. He blesses us that we may be a blessing to others. Your gift (ability) is not for you. It will benefit you, but it's not for you. It's always to bless someone else. This book, my speaking, my traveling and teaching others is not for me. It's for those who see me, hear me and read the words that God gives me to write. Doing these things benefit me and my family because I earn an income, but make no mistake, my gift is not for me. That gift that's inside of you is for someone else as well. It's for me. People are waiting on you. There are people in this world that only you will be able to touch, reach and help. No one else can do it. ONLY YOU!

If you're in business, get excited. If you're in a relationship, get excited. Excitement is contagious. Remember how my excitement about AmeriPlan got Erin involved and on board? Customers can tell when an employee or business owner is excited about what they're doing. It makes them want to come back again and again. There's nothing worse than walking into a business and the person behind the counter has a bad attitude. No excitement in sight. No smiles, no joy, no nothing. We have all been in a place like this haven't we? You probably thought of a place just then when I described it, didn't you? I hate to stereotype, but here it goes anyway. Think about the major difference in attitude and excitement between most fast food chains and Chick-fil-A. I have never had bad service or experienced bad attitudes at Chick-fil-A. Why? What's the secret? Tell me! Please! They seem to always be excited.

When people think of your business, what's the first thought that comes to their mind? Is it the Chick-fil-A experience? What about at home? Is it the Chick-fil-A experience? At one point in our life, Erin and I were not excited about our relationship. Neither one of us wanted to be here. And just like customers can tell, so can children. We both decided that we wanted to make a change. We were no longer willing to accept things the way they were, and we wanted a change. So we went to work.

We sought counseling from those who invested in our relationship. We cut ties with those friends who were speaking negative about the other spouse. We went on date nights, we communicated (MEN, TALK TO YOUR WIVES), we laughed, we got excited and we are making it work. If you are willing to turn your relationship and your business over to God, you can make it too. God is not a respecter of persons. He doesn't play favorites. If He did it for us, He can do it for you as well.

Now, I don't always get it right. At times I can still have a bad attitude. Yes…even me! When I tell people this, they don't believe me. They say that Steve Wilmer always has a positive attitude. He is always happy, energetic, motivational, blah, blah, blah. Don't believe everything in the bio. As a matter of fact, I was recycled, held back in Marine Corps boot camp for having a bad attitude. My wife Erin has to put me in check from time to time because of my attitude with my family. She says that my family should get the best of Steve Wilmer and not the leftovers. She is absolutely right. Let's make sure we give our very best to our families first. They see us at our very worst and still support us in spite of ourselves.

I said earlier that excitement is contagious, but so is a bad attitude. And it starts with the leader. It was Art Williams who said, "People won't follow a dull, boring, negative cry-baby." If employees have a bad attitude, take a closer look at the employer. If a family has a bad attitude, take a closer look at the head (leader). Get excited about what you're doing. Find a way

Now it's pretty obvious that this person has a very bad

to make it work, be willing to do the hard work or find something else to do.

It's been said that life is 1% of what happens to us and 99% of how we respond to it. It's all in how we view things. This was shared with me recently, and I think it brings the point home of what attitude is all about:

Worst Day Ever
by Chanie Gorkin

> TODAY WAS THE ABSOLUTE WORST DAY EVER
> AND DON'T TRY TO CONVINCE ME THAT
> THERE'S SOMETHING GOOD IN EVERY DAY
> BECAUSE WHEN YOU TAKE A CLOSER LOOK
> THE WORLD IS A PRETTY BAD PLACE
> EVEN IF
> SOME GOODNESS DOES SHINE THROUGH ONCE IN A WHILE
> SATISFACTION AND HAPPINESS DOESN'T LAST
> AND IT'S NOT TRUE THAT
> IT'S ALL IN YOUR MIND AND HEART
> BECAUSE
> TRUE HAPPINESS CAN BE OBTAINED
> ONLY IF YOUR SURROUNDINGS ARE GOOD
> IT'S NOT TRUE THAT GOOD EXISTS
> I'M SURE YOU CAN AGREE THAT
> MY REALITY
> CREATES
> MY ATTITUDE
> IT'S ALL BEYOND MY CONTROL
> AND YOU'LL NEVER IN A MILLION YEARS HEAR ME SAY THAT
> TODAY WAS A GOOD DAY

Now it's pretty obvious that this person has a very bad attitude, a negative attitude. Imagine that this is your employee. Imagine that this is your child or spouse. Imagine that this is you. We are not a product of our circumstances. We are a product of our decisions correct? We all can decide how we respond and how we view things. For example, read "Worst Day Ever" one more time. But this time read it backwards, from the bottom to the top. Like this, "Today was a good day and you'll never in a million years hear me say that it's all..."

Wow, how about that? Two people can see the exact same thing and view it totally different. Remember this passage the next time an unfortunate circumstance happens at work or at home. You have a choice as to how you view it. I worked for the John Kizziah State Farm Agency for years. John was a great leader of our team. Early in my insurance career, whenever there was a rate increase, making it a little more difficult to sell policies, we, the team, would often get upset and start complaining. John would simply say to us, "Team, we control what we can control." I was watching his attitude towards the situation. If he would have complained, there is no doubt that we would have followed suit and continued with our negative attitude. But he didn't, so neither did we. As I now travel the country training other agencies how to sell insurance, I find myself saying to them, "You control what you can control."

Thanks, John. Remember that our employees and family members are also watching to see how we respond.

Working for John, I was one of the top insurance salesmen in my area. I was very good at what I did and I enjoyed what I did. I looked forward to helping all of my customers each and every day. I did not have that sickening feeling in my stomach on Sunday night. I was definitely not a clock watcher. But it really wasn't my passion. I have been teaching, training and speaking for the last ten years for free. That's when you know that you are passionate about something. You will do it even if you are not paid to do so. It wasn't until I left the insurance field and began traveling and teaching that I realized this. I had been preparing to be an insurance agent for years.

If I'm completely honest with myself, it's only because I felt that being an insurance agent was safe. I could do it easily and it wouldn't require much risk. How many times do we play it safe? How many times do we take the easy road? The safe route? No one ever accomplished anything great by taking the easy road. Robert Frost said, "Two roads diverged in a wood, and I-I took the one less traveled by, And that has made all the difference." Ask yourself, "Am I making a difference? Am I following my passion?" If the answer is no, ask yourself, "Why not?"

I'm 47 years old, and I just made a major career change (again) in order to be a speaker, trainer and author because this is my passion. I wake up in the morning thinking about it; I go to bed at night thinking about it. At times, I go all day long without eating. I'm telling you, there is nothing like living your passion. Are you passionate about what you're doing? Do you really enjoy what you're doing? If the answer is yes, then great. Keep doing it and work as unto the Lord. But If the answer is no, then make a change. Do what you love to do. Get all the information required. Do your homework so that you will make an informed decision. Pray about it first. Get an answer from God. Talk to your spouse about it as well. Make this important decision together.

Now, if you're not doing what you're passionate about, don't get down on yourself. I've got good news for you. It's not too late to change.

#2 **In order to Win in Life & Business, you have to get excited about what you're doing. Follow your passion and work as unto the Lord.**

4 Steps of Effective Decision Making:

1. Stop: Stop what you're doing, find a quiet place, get rid of the noise, clear your mind, relax and focus.

2. Ask the right questions from the right people: Get advice from someone succeeding in the area that you are considering; consult with an expert. Sometimes, the right people are not family members or friends. They love you, but they are often fearful themselves.

3. Think about the consequences/rewards: What happens if I do/don't? What could I lose/gain? What are the pros/cons?

4. Respond accordingly: Respond to your findings and make a decision. I did not say make the right decision. Unfortunately, you may not find this out until years later. Respond, don't react. We always go wrong when we react.

"Catch on fire with enthusiasm and people will come for miles to watch you burn." - John Wesley

"Nothing great was ever achieved without enthusiasm."
-Ralph Waldo Emerson

"10 To Win"

<u>Notes:</u>

CHAPTER 3
PUSH OR PULL
"10 To Win"

The MCCRES (Marine Corps Combat Readiness Evaluation System) was designed to test the combat effectiveness of Marine Corps Infantry Units. Part of the MCCRES evaluation includes a 25-mile hump, also referred to as a death march, in full gear from point "A" to "B" within 8 hours or less. The time had come for my unit, Golf Company 2nd Battalion, 2nd Marines 2nd Marine Division, to perform the MCCRES.

I was not looking forward to this hump. Many of the older Marines in my platoon, referred to as salty dogs, had done this in the past, and they were telling stories about how people have passed out and not been able to complete the march. I was nervous to say the least, but I was also determined that I would complete this march. The night before the march, I made sure that my gear was packed tightly and ready to go. I made sure to hit the rack (bed) early and get a good night's sleep. Reveille (time to wake up) was at 0500 (5 a.m.), and the march was to begin at 0630.

The next morning came quickly as I jumped out of my rack upon hearing the alarm clock. I hit the head (restroom), washed up, got dressed; and my roommate and I were out the door to the chow hall for a quick bite to eat. There was dew on the ground from the morning fog, and I could see the sky starting to light up in the east from the rising sun. The North Carolina air was fresh and crisp. The temperature was perfect this September morning. I thought to myself, "What a great day for a death march." We finished chow and headed back to the barracks to get ready. Our sergeants were coming around to make sure that we were ready to go as well.

One of my sergeants was Kenny Green. He was a southern boy from South Carolina. Before the Marine Corps, he had been a martial arts instructor. He'd won some tournaments, and his nickname was "Sweet Feet". At times, he would demonstrate some karate moves for us. He was extremely fast. We all joked, "You don't mess with Sgt. Green." He was always squared away, demonstrating great military bearing. Every time you saw him, he had a smile on his face; and when he spoke to you, he did not use foul language. Foul language was commonplace in the infantry unit. I was a young Marine (18), and I admired and respected Sgt. Green. He was one of the first male figures in my life that I viewed as a leader.

It was now time to head to formation and begin this march. The sun was now peeking through the clouds as Golf Company, approximately 156 Marines, formed up for this death march. The Captain said a few words of encouragement to us; there was some Marine Corps yelling from the excitement, none by me of course, and off we went.

We wasted no time getting into a quick rhythm. One foot in front of the other over and over again. It was an extremely brisk pace, and we had to stay together as a unit, packed tightly, with very little space between each man. My pack sat high on my back and my Squad Automatic Weapon (SAW), was slung around my neck. I could see Sgt. Green up ahead of me, turning around from time to time encouraging us to, "Keep it tight." Initially, we all joked and talked as we were marching, attempting to take our minds off of the task at hand. We took breaks, drank water and snacked on fruit from the chow hall. It had to be around mile 10 when I started to feel it. You would be surprised at how the simplest things can bother you after a while. For instance, I'd never noticed that my right foot slid forward ever so slightly inside my boot when my socks were wet. My SAW only weighed 18lbs but after 10 miles, being slung around my neck, it felt like an anchor.

At this point, there was a lot less talking and joking among us. My head was down, just looking at the pair of boots moving forward in front of me. My mind drifted off to more pleasant things. I thought about my high school graduation the year before. I wondered what my friends were doing at this very moment. I also thought, "What in the world have I gotten myself into?" I was a little dazed, but I could still hear Sgt. Green up in front of me, "Let's go Marines. Keep it tight, Ooh Rah Marine Corps." There was grumbling from others about Sgt. Green's enthusiasm but no one dared say a word to him out loud. Remember, "You don't mess with Sgt. Green."

At mile 20, it was extremely bad for a lot of us. Some Marines had already dropped out. I had taken my SAW from around my neck, and I was now carrying it by the barrel, leaning against my shoulder. My pack was starting to dig into my back with each movement that I made. My feet were throbbing and aching with each step that I took, especially my right foot. It was extremely painful every time I planted my foot on the ground. I could feel a blister forming on the bottom of my foot. My camouflage top

SAW - Squad Automatic Weapon

was soaked with sweat from the sun, and my helmet felt like a cast iron skillet sitting on top of my head. I was sure that I wouldn't finish this march. This was by far the hardest single thing I'd ever done in my short life span. I could hear other sergeants in the rear yelling at Marines to keep up and stay in formation. I was fearful at their words. I knew that it would be me that they would be yelling at soon. God had mercy on me and the captain called for our last break before the home stretch.

Marine Corps Death March

We all slumped to the ground in pain and anguish. I grabbed my canteen and began drinking water vigorously. I was done. I was not going to get up and finish this march. There was no way that I could. I'd gone as far as I felt I could go. I then heard a familiar voice, "Wilmer, are you okay?" I looked up. It was Sgt. Green. "I can't do this," I replied. He said, "Yes, you can Marine. You can do this. We are almost there." I began to tell him about my foot, my back, my legs, my head, EVERYTHING.

He said, "Wilmer, I'm hurting too. My feet hurt, my back hurts as well. I want to quit also, but I'm going to finish this march and you will too. Your body is lying to you. It's telling you that you can't go any further, but you can. Just keep your eyes on me. When I quit, then you can quit." I have remembered those words ever since. "Your body is lying to you." To this day, anytime I've done anything physical and wanted to quit, I hear Sgt. Green's words and I continue moving forward. He was right.

Break time was now over, and we were back at it again. I stood to my feet, wondering how much farther I could go before I gave up. We began moving, step by step, same fast pace. I was about to give up when I heard that familiar voice again, "Wilmer, are you watching me? Let's go Marine." Initially, I thought that this was crazy. What would watching him do? But as I began to watch him, I began to draw from his strength. My eyes stayed focused on him step by step, mile by mile. "Wilmer, are you still watching?" Sgt. Green would yell from time to time. Tired and dazed, I replied, "Yes." When he moved, I moved. If he had stopped, I would have stopped, but he didn't stop. There was also a part of me that didn't want to let him down. He was my leader and he was counting on me to finish the job. Finally, we made it to our destination with time to spare.

After the captain addressed us and congratulated us on

a job well done, he dismissed us. I immediately dropped my pack to the ground and sat down right where we were, along with half the company. I closed my eyes and felt like I was going to die of exhaustion. Above me, I heard a familiar voice once again. "Wilmer, are you okay?" I replied, saying, "Yes I'm okay." He then said, "Good job, Marine. I told you that you could do it." As Sgt. Green walked away, I remember thinking to myself, "He was right. My body said that I couldn't go another step. I was sure of it. But I did go another step. I went another five miles. I kept my eyes on my leader, and I accomplished the task. Thank you, Sgt. Green. Here's the funny thing: as I was sitting there exhausted, the Marine next to me said, "Wilmer, I was behind you the whole time. I wanted to give up a long time ago, but I just kept looking down at your boots. You kept moving, so I kept moving." Wow! I had no idea that someone was looking at me for their strength. Unbeknownst to me, I was a leader.

When I think of leaders, who made a positive impression on my life, Sgt. Kenny "Sweet Feet" Green is at the top of that list. Ask yourself, am I a good leader? What if your employees were asked that question, how would they respond? If your co-workers were asked that question, how would they answer it? What if your family was asked that question, would they agree that you are a good leader? There are lots of books and articles and definitions about leadership and what it takes to be a good leader. There's so much information on this subject that it hurts my head to try to encompass it all. It's information overload. My best definition of a leader is someone who inspires you to accomplish the task at hand, and then shows you how it's done. The inspiration may come in many different forms, but their actions or words make you want to do something. In my book, that's a leader.

Business owners, do your actions or words inspire your employees to want to accomplish the mission? Do they feel empowered when they see you and listen to you? Or are they fearful of the consequences if they don't accomplish the mission? Which is it? Of course, you can say, "Well, I pay them to do a job, and that's what I expect them to do. If they want inspiration, let them watch the movie "Rudy" or go to a motivation seminar to hear Steve Wilmer speak. That is your right as a business owner. But if that's your attitude, then you are not a leader but rather a "Boss"; and the two are nothing alike.

Don't be mistaken! The same principles apply within your family. This was a hard lesson for me to learn, and I'm still learning every day. My mother barked orders when she wanted me to do something. Often there were no words of inspiration or affirmation. She raised me the best way that she knew how. I'm sure she got it from her mother as well. In Judah's earlier days, I barked orders at him as well. There was no inspiration.

It was my way or the highway. I had to learn to be a leader in my home rather than a boss. People will follow a leader out of respect and admiration, but they will fear a boss. Fear breeds hatred and no loyalty. Respect breeds love and loyalty.

As a father, I want my family to love me, respect me and be loyal to me. I would want the same as a business owner. If this is your desired destination, then you must become a leader, not a boss. As I was marching and wanted to give up, I could hear the "bosses" behind me yelling at other Marines. I was fearful, but I was still going to give up. The leader, Sgt. Green was in front of me encouraging me to continue, and I accomplished the task. If you want people to accomplish a task, then become a leader and not a boss.

Here's an age old question for you? Are leaders made or born? I've had plenty of discussion on this subject at my seminars. The answer is that there are no wrong answers to this question. It's simply a matter of opinion, and there will always be an example for either side. I personally believe that leaders are made. There's all kind of trainings and seminars on leadership. I've even conducted my share on the subject. I was not a leader growing up or in school. The Marine Corps was my first class on leadership. And when I became a Non-Commissioned Officer, I received a crash course on leading men to accomplish the mission. I do believe that some people are born with certain leadership traits within them. Those traits have to be brought out, discovered and nurtured so as to make them flourish. That's why it's considered such a compliment when someone says, "They're a natural born leader." It's because most leaders are made, not born.

I chose the title "Push or Pull" for this chapter for one reason only. Logistics! Any time you want to move something forward, you have a decision to make: You can either get behind it and push it forward, or you can get in front of it and pull it forward. One day while working on my "honey do" list, Erin needed me to move the living room table. It's big, square and made of marble. I got on one side of the table and pulled it towards me, inch by inch. It took a little longer, but I got the job done. When it was time to put the table back, I didn't want to work that hard, so rather than going to the opposite side and pulling it back, I took a short cut. I pushed the table back into place. It was easier and quicker, but I scratched the floor.

You see, a boss pushes people around. A boss is always behind the people and never in front of them, always commanding and demanding, instilling fear, scratching and hurting the people. It's easy to be a boss. It's a lot harder to pull something. A leader pulls people forward through inspiration, leading the way, always out in the front, always asking and having dialogue, earning respect from his or her followers and not hurting the people. It takes a considerable amount of effort to be a leader.

You've likely seen the picture that seems to show an ancient Egyptian hieroglyphic. On the top there are 3 men pulling, and 1 man sitting on a large block with a desk on top. With a caption above his head that reads, "Boss". Below that image is a picture with 4 men pulling the large block with the man who was on the block now leading the way pulling the block. It has a caption that reads, "Leader". I believe this image demonstrates the core difference between a boss and a leader.

BOSS	**LEADER**
Drives Employees	**Coaches Employees**
Instills Fear	**Generates Enthusiasm**
Says "I"	**Says "We"**
Places Blame	**Works on a Solution**
Knows how to do it	**Shows how to do it**
Takes all the credit	**Gives all the credit**
Commands	**Asks**
Says "Go"	**Says "Let's Go"**

Become a leader in your home and your place of work. As I mentioned in my Marine Corps story above, sometimes you may not be aware that someone else is watching you as an example. You may not be aware that you are leading others, inspiring others. Matthew 5:16 says, *"Let your light shine before others, that they may see your good deeds and glorify your Father in heaven."* Take a moment to reflect on some of the leaders who have had a positive impact on your life. Also, ask yourself, would someone be thinking of you if they read this?

    Let's take a look at a few good leaders from history. I say "good" because there are some leaders who have used their influence for bad things. What kind of influence are you? A few years ago my daughter Jayna, who loves to sing, had to be about four years old. We were all sitting at the dinner table, and she began singing a rap song. Erin and I looked at each other in shock. "Where did you hear that?" We both asked her in a disgusted tone. Without hesitation, Jayna said, "Daddy." If looks could kill, I would not be here to write this book. Upon further investigation, we discovered that Jayna heard the song on the radio while I was taking her to school that morning. Now that's a simple and probably harmless example. But it goes to show you that even the simplest of things can have an influence on others. Let's be ever mindful of this, especially when it comes to our children. The old attitude of, "Do what I say and not what I do," doesn't work. Be a positive influence on those around you. Be a good leader. Incidentally, we don't listen to the radio anymore while driving to school.

Push or Pull

Let's evaluate a few leaders.

General George Washington was the Commander-in-Chief of the Continental Army during the American Revolutionary War, and one of the Founding Fathers of the United States. He also became the first president of the United States and was called the "father of our country."

Anna "Eleanor" Roosevelt was an American politician, diplomat, and activist. She was the longest-serving and one of the most active first ladies in history, working for political, racial and social justice.

Vincent "Vince" Lombardi was best known as the head coach of the Green Bay Packers. He led his team to three straight and five total National Football League championships in seven years, including the first two Super Bowls. He is considered to be one of the best and most successful coaches in professional football history.

Nelson Mandela was a South African anti-apartheid revolutionary. After serving 27 years in prison, he was released and elected as the country's first president in a fully representative democratic election. His administration tackled institutionalized racism and fostered racial reconciliation.

And of course, the greatest leader of them all was Jesus

Christ, the Son of the living God. He walked this earth over 2000 years ago and yet still has more followers around the world than anyone else. His teachings are chronicled in the Bible and have saved many lives. His death and resurrection make it possible for all mankind to live with Him forever in Heaven by accepting Him as our Lord and Savior.

Let's talk briefly about some characteristics of a good leader.

Vision: A good leader always knows where he or she is headed, and they have a plan to get there. They share their vision with their followers so that everyone is on the same page. They accept help and solicit input to carry out their vision. A good leader is also not afraid to change directions if they find that their plan is not working. Matthew 4:19 *"And he (Jesus) said to them, follow me and I will make you fishers of men."*

Servant: A good leader is also a servant. He or she is not lifted up in pride. They are humble. They don't mind getting their hands dirty. A good leader will never ask you to do something that they aren't willing to do themselves. They give their all. John 13:5 says, *"After that, he (Jesus) poured water into a basin and began to wash his disciples' feet."*

Inspiring: A good leader inspires those around them. They speak positive things into other's lives. They teach, train, coach and also challenge their followers so that they will become better. Mark 1:22 says, *"The people were amazed at his teaching because he taught them as one who had authority."*

Sacrifice: A good leader makes sacrifices for their followers. Often, they will go without, to make sure that those depending on them have their needs met. This past Christmas holiday, Erin's office had to remain open, so she went to work on Christmas Eve so that her employees could stay home with their families. I may be biased, but I think this was an example of a good leader. No doubt she learned this while serving 24 years in the US Navy. John 10:11 says, *"I am the good shepherd. The good shepherd lays down his life for the sheep."*

If you are the head of an organization, be it a business, church, family, etc., be a leader, not a boss. Inspire and encourage those following you. Lead by example--from the front and not from behind. It may be a little more difficult, but the reward is well worth it. Take your cues from the greatest leader of all time. You won't always get it right, but be quick to ask for forgiveness and keep moving forward. Remember to "pull" rather than "push."

#3 IN ORDER TO WIN IN LIFE & BUSINESS, YOU HAVE TO BE A LEADER. PROMOTE ENTHUSIASM RATHER THAN FEAR TO THOSE FOLLOWING YOU. LEAD BY EXAMPLE, FROM THE FRONT.

"When I talk to a boss, I get the feeling that they are important. When I talk to a leader, I get the feeling that I am important." - Howard Farran

"Leaders become great, not because of their power, but because of their ability to empower others." - John Maxwell

Notes:

CHAPTER 4

Pump Your Brakes

"10 To Win"

Every year, the John Kizziah Agency had certain goals we strived to attain. Author and speaker, Zig Ziglar said, "You can have everything in life that you want if you will help enough people get what they want." This was our philosophy, to help as many of our customers obtain the insurance coverage that they wanted. For years, one of those "wants" was health insurance. After the Affordable Care Act was passed, we had the opportunity to help our customers with this important benefit. Customers only had a short window (Nov. 15 – Dec. 15) in which to enroll to have health insurance at the beginning of the year.

During our weekly team meeting, we discussed our goal. It was to help twenty of our customers get enrolled during this 30-day period. Stephanie Noto-Slack was in charge of health and she made sure that our goal was clearly defined. I would be remiss if I didn't acknowledge that it was Stephanie who initially trained me to be an insurance agent. She is an amazing instructor and good friend. Thanks Steph! But why did we have this goal? We discussed this as well to make sure that everyone was on the same page and understood why we were doing what we were doing.

First, as I said earlier, it would help our customers, and by helping our customers, it would also help us reach our annual health premium number. Next, everyone had to agree on the goal. If anyone disagreed, we discussed the reason and gave them an opportunity to remove themselves from the responsibility and rewards for achieving the goal. After we discussed this, we went around the table and talked about the things we all would receive, individually, if we achieved our goal. We talked about things such as, "helping our customers meet their needs, the feeling of agency pride because we were always competing with other agencies, and of course, the commissions and bonuses that we would receive from the sales."

Once we finished discussing these things, we then came up with a plan on how we were going to accomplish our goal. We had fun brainstorming and came up with 8-10 different ideas. Everyone participated and provided input. We narrowed those down to 3 solid ideas that we knew we could implement to yield the best results. We were all on the same page, so we went to work, putting our plan into action.

Everyone had a specific assignment and each week we

kept track and made sure that we were all completing that assignment. When the 30-day enrollment period was over, we discussed our results at our next team meeting. Our goal was to help twenty customers get enrolled with health insurance. We helped over forty get enrolled. Thanks to everyone's effort, and Stephanie's leadership, we achieved our goal. We doubled the annual premium we needed, and we were number 1 in our sales territory. Our office was ecstatic at our results. It goes to show that when you make SMART goals, it enhances your chances of success. Way to go Team Kizziah! (John, Stephanie, Jennifer, Tricia, Krissy, Angela, Beth, Chase & Aaron)

John Kizziah Team - StateFarm

In this chapter, I would like to focus on the process that you use when setting your goals. Let's begin with a simple explanation of a goal. A goal is the desired result that a person or a system envisions, plans and commits to achieve. We should all have results that we commit to achieving in our life and business; therefore, we should have goals already set in these two areas. Review your goal and make sure that it is a SMART goal.

S. Our goals should be specific, not all over the place. If we are selling widgets, our goal shouldn't be to sell as many widgets as possible. The goal should have a specific number so that we know whether or not we achieved it. Our goal in this example was 20. It would have been easier to say, "As many as possible." If we did that and wrote 19 or 10 or even 1, we would have achieved our so-called goal and then told ourselves that was all that was possible. Since we set a number, a benchmark, we knew whether or not we achieved it. At times, we would also have a stretch goal. For example, our goal is 20, and our stretch goal is 30. How will we know what we can achieve unless we reach for the stars? Remember the death march in Chapter 3? 25 miles in 8 hours was the goal, rather than as far as we can go. Specific goals punch us right in the face. They let us know if we are cutting the mustard or not. There's no guessing when our goals are specific.

M. Our goals should be motivational and measurable. Goal setting should be fun. It should be inspiring to talk about the future benefits of achieving the goal. Everyone should be involved in the process, and that includes employees or family members. Everyone should feel like they have a say in ways to accomplish the goal. It's no fun when one person comes up with the goal and the best way to go about accomplishing it.

The goal should also be measurable as well. This is a big one. Unfortunately, most organizations and families measure their results against others. I disagree with this method. Someone else's result only tells you that the result itself is possible to achieve. We should measure our results by yesterday. Are we better than we were yesterday? Did we sell more widgets than we sold yesterday? If we keep improving on our results, we will attain our goal, not someone else's.

A. Our goal should be attainable and accountable. I mentioned having a stretch goal earlier. Sometimes we set goals that are out of our reach for the time being. If we set SMART goals, we will eventually hit those benchmarks, but we all must crawl before we can walk. The danger in setting unattainable goals is that it constantly makes your team/family feel like they are failures. We all must experience some victories in our life.

And let's not be afraid to hold one another accountable for our portion of making sure that the goal is met. We all know that a chain is only as strong as its weakest link. There is team accountability, and there is personal accountability. Both should work hand in hand to make sure that we are moving forward to accomplish the same mission. You may even want to tell someone, like an outsider, about your goal and have them hold you accountable as well. But teams most certainly fail when there is no accountability.

R. Our goal should be responsible and relevant. Our goal should never put anyone at risk, physically, emotionally or otherwise. Our bodies need rest, and our families need our time, so no goal should ever cause physical or emotional damage to us or others. I am reminded about the pizza chain who years ago had a goal of "pizza delivered in 30 minutes or less, or it's free." That goal was allegedly the cause of a child's death in a vehicle accident.

Our goals must be relevant to the situation at hand. Enrolling our customers with health insurance was directly related to the passing of the Affordable Care Act. It would have been irrelevant to focus on home owner's insurance during these particular 30 days.

T. Our goal should have a timeline. Remember, a goal without a timeline is nothing more than a wish. Our timeline to enroll our customers was 30 days. The rules dictated the timeline for us. Often, we must decide our own timeline. The best way to determine the timeline is to look at the four steps above, and they should help determine a reasonable timeline. Our team kept a public calendar so that we all could see exactly where we were and how much time we had left to accomplish our goal. Goals require timelines.

Once you set your SMART goal, the next thing to do is figure out how you will go about accomplishing your goal. The problem is that once we have our goal in mind, most of us are like a Porsche 911 Turbo. We go from 0 to 60 in 2.9 seconds. We say, "Here is the goal, now how am I going to accomplish it?" We miss three very important steps in this process. If we want buy-in from our team and our family, we should make sure that they are on the same page with the same goal in mind. After we all establish the goal, we should explain why we have this goal in the first place. What are the benefits and who will it help?

Next we want agreement on the goal from those involved. Unless we have an agreement, we shouldn't move forward. Amos 3:3 says, *"Can two walk together unless they agree to do so?"* Agreement is one element that I have not seen in any goal setting books. Usually the person in charge says what the goal is, and everyone else follows.

Once we have agreement from the participants, let's tune in to everyone's favorite radio station, WIIFM, and talk about "what's in it for me?" Have fun discussing what you will receive from achieving the goal. If it's money, talk about some of the things that you will do with the money.

Lastly, let's brainstorm and come up with ways to accomplish the goal. Everyone who agreed to the goal participates in this process and in the rewards when the goal is met. There are no wrong answers or stupid ideas. Write them all down. Then go back and pick two or three ideas that you can reasonably implement. This process will take considerable more time than the other way, but we will have a team that's on the same page. So before you decide on how you will accomplish your next goal, "Pump Your Brakes", take your time, and use this process instead.

Does it work with family? You may ask. Why, yes it does. All parents want their children to do well in school. Unfortunately, the conversation between parent and child goes something like this, "Study hard so you will do well in school." The goal is to do well in school. The how is to study hard. 0 to 60 in 2.9 seconds. Been there, done that. My children attend Trinitas Christian School. They receive a classical Christian education. The school gives academic awards at the end of every school year to those students who excel in their studies. One year my daughter Joi decided that she wanted to receive an academic award. That was her goal. I asked why she wanted to receive the award. She stated that she wanted to make us proud, and she really wanted that award. I told her what achieving the award would require from her and asked if she agreed to do the work. She agreed, and Erin and I agreed to help her. I then told her that if she did receive the award, I would give her $50 and take

Pump Your Brakes

her to the toy store and let her pick out a toy. You should have seen the look on her face. I asked her to tell me some of the toys she would consider buying. It appeared that she would need a little more money than $50.

We then came up with a plan on how to get this done. Mom would help her study and test her on certain days while I would help her on the other days. Joi put in the work and never let up. At the end of the school year, Joi received her Cum Laude award. She bought into the goal because I involved her in the process, rather than speeding through "Pump Your Brakes" and telling her what to do. FYI, I'm still working on that oldest boy. Please pray for me. It just goes to show that for this to work out as planned, you must have agreement and buy-in from those involved in achieving the goal.

*Joi Wilmer
Cum Lade Award*

#4 In order to Win in Life and Business, you have to set SMART goals. Take your time and don't rush through the process.

REMEMBER TO PUMP YOUR BRAKES.

"People with goals succeed, because they know where they're going."
- Earl Nightingale

The tragedy of life doesn't lie in not reaching your goals. The tragedy lies in having no goals to reach."
-Benjamin Mays

<u>Notes:</u>

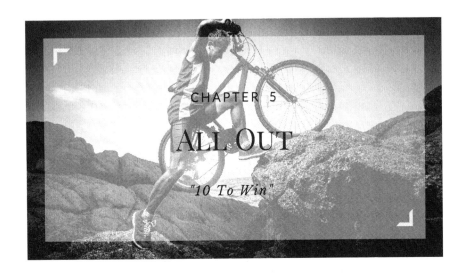

CHAPTER 5
ALL OUT
"10 To Win"

In the movie Star Wars, <u>The Empire Strikes Back</u>, Luke Skywalker is running through the swamp with Master Yoda on his back. Luke is in training to become a Jedi. As Luke is turning flips and climbing vines, Yoda is talking in Luke's ear giving him instructions on how to use the force and stay away from the dark side. During one part of his training, Luke is doing a one-armed handstand, both feet in the air, spread apart with Yoda standing on the bottom of one of Luke's feet, while Luke moves large stones with his mind (the force) and stacks them next to him. In the distance, Luke sees his spaceship starting to sink into the murky swamp water. Luke panics and loses his focus. First, the rocks fall, and then Luke falls; and, of course, Yoda falls.

Luke gets up, brushes himself off, looks at his sinking spaceship and makes the comment, "We'll never get it out now." Yoda replies (in only the way that Yoda can), "So certain are you?" Yoda appears disappointed in Luke's negative comment and his negative attitude. Yoda drops his head in frustration and says to Luke, "Always with you, it cannot be done." Luke tells Yoda that moving stones is different than moving a spaceship. Yoda replies that the only difference is in your mind. Yoda then goes on to say some of the most powerful words ever spoken on the movie screen. He tells Luke, "You must unlearn what you have learned." Luke half-heartedly listens to Yoda and unconvincingly says, "All right, I'll give it a try." Yoda quickly and sternly says, "No, try not." "Do, or do not. There is no try."

Anytime I am asked to provide my biography during a speaking engagement, those words, "Do or do not, there is no try" are always at the bottom of the page, as what I consider to be my secret to success. It's actually not a secret at all. It's something that people discovered a long time ago. When you put your mind to something, work hard and don't give up, you will most likely achieve the results you want.

The first thing that I see is that Luke was doing fine focusing on the hand-stand, focusing on stacking the rocks and focusing on not dropping Master Yoda. He was doing a great job at what he was focused on. What you think about and focus on most always becomes your maximum potential. When Luke began focusing on his ship, everything started to fall apart. This principle happens in business and life all the time. We are going along doing great, and something or someone gets us off focus. They get our attention off what it should be on. Now please be careful because it's important to keep the main thing as the main thing. I don't want to get ahead of myself, but the main thing is not your business. You will read more about this in Chapter 10.

There are more important things in this world than money. Now don't get me wrong, money is important. Anyone who says that money is not important probably has too much or too little of it. Mark 8:36 says, *"For what shall it profit a man, if he shall gain the whole world, and lose his soul?"* Folks, there will always be a sinking ship. Sometimes, it's not even our ship. The ship belongs to someone else, and we allow our world to fall apart trying to save someone else's ship. There is nothing wrong with helping others. I mentioned one of my favorite Zig Ziglar quotes earlier, "If you help enough people get what they want, then you can have everything that you want." That's a great quote. A Polish Proverb reads, "Every time you feel yourself being pulled into other people's drama, repeat these words, not my circus, not my monkeys." We don't have to get involved in everyone's problems.

I find myself saying this to my wife often. Erin has a good heart and is always trying to help everyone who asks for help. She is always telling me about someone else's problems. At times, if she is not careful, she will begin to stress about someone else's sinking ship, and this will cause our ship to start rocking.

Everybody's problem is not your problem. Lend a hand if and when you can, but don't let someone's ship sink your ship, or get you off focus, no matter who they are. If they truly loved and cared for you and your well-being, then they would not drag you onboard their sinking ship, their burning house or their issues of life. Sometimes people genuinely need and deserve our help. However, most of the time, they are simply selfish and only care about themselves. So get focused, get back on track and take care of what needs to be taken care of.

Sometimes good things can get us off focus. Yes, good things. We volunteer our time and become involved in worthy causes, but those causes distract us. We join this organization and that organization, diluting our time. There was a point when I was involved in just about every networking group in Pensacola. I had to learn to step back, resign my positions, and regain my focus. I had to join the NAVY (Never Again Volunteer Yourself). Do you need to join the NAVY as well?

The next thing that I notice in this scene is that Yoda had to deal with Luke's negative words, "We'll never get it out now." How many times do we speak negatives words over ourselves, our business, our family, and even our children? We say things like: "It can't be done or I can't do it; I can't win for losing; I'll always be in debt, in the red, and can't keep good employees; My family doesn't care, and my children won't listen." One negative word after another comes out of our mouths. Proverbs 18:21 says, *"The power of death and life is in the tongue?"* You shall have what you say. If you speak negative things over your situation, you shall receive negative results. I want you to start speaking LIFE over your family and your business. Regardless of what things look like, start to speak how you want things to be rather than how they are.

At this beginning stage, you don't have to believe what you're saying "yet." I just want you to start training yourself to speak positive vs. negative, life vs. death, success vs. failure. Once you began to speak it, you will train yourself to expect it, and then you will begin to believe it. You would be surprised at how positive words can affect your life for good. Remember, you have to see it before you see it.

"The only difference is in your mind," Yoda says to Luke when Luke compares moving stones with moving a spaceship. How many times do we defeat ourselves in our mind before ever trying to do something? Yoda was trying to tell Luke that if you can move a stone with your mind, then you can move a spaceship. There is no difference. It's called faith. If you have the faith to move a stone, you have the faith to move a spaceship. If you have the faith to move a spaceship, you have the faith to move a mountain and have it cast into the sea. My son, Judah asked me one day, "Dad, which is heavier, a pound of feathers or a pound of iron?" Immediately, my mind wants to say that the iron is heavier than the feathers. But that would be untrue because they are both the same. There is no difference. The only difference is in your mind. If you can have five employees, then you can have fifty. You may not want fifty, but don't allow your mind to tell you it's not possible. If you can own one store, then you can own two. If you can earn X income this year, then you can earn XXX income next year. Everything is possible to those that believe. It's all in your mind. If you don't mind, it doesn't matter.

Yoda goes on to tell Luke that he must "unlearn" what he has learned. How powerful is this statement? Ask yourself, what have I learned? What have I been taught? What have I been taught about business? What have I been taught about family? What have I been taught about myself? Most importantly, who taught me? If you know the story, Luke grew up with his uncle and aunt who were simple people. They were not warriors or fighters. So they taught Luke to be a simple person as well and to live a simple life. So that's what he did until he met Ben Obi Wan Kenobi.

SPOILER ALERT!

For those of you who have been "living in a cave" and never saw the Star Wars trilogy, it turns out that Luke is the son of Darth Vader, one of the most powerful characters in the movie. Luke already had the "force" inside of him, certain hidden abilities on the inside of him, certain powers on the inside of him. But because he was never taught this, he lived a simple and somewhat defeated life.

We all have to unlearn some things that we have learned. When I was young, I learned that the father is not supposed to be in the home with the children and mother. I learned that it was normal to have your utilities turned off for non-payment. I learned that it's normal for roaches and rats to be prevalent in the home. I even learned that I'm not supposed to own a home. When I was in high school, I learned from one of my teachers that I would never amount to anything. Most of the time, experience is our teacher (I did not say the best teacher) and we accept the lessons it delivers. You should never follow advice from anyone on any subject matter unless they are an expert in that particular area.

One of the books that changed my life was <u>Rich Dad Poor Dad</u> by Robert Kiyosaki. It helped me unlearn what I learned about school, employees, business and being rich. Robert's rich dad was a high school dropout while his poor dad was a college professor. You should read the book. My uncle Charles Packer helped me unlearn what I learned about family, fathers, responsibility, and a man's role in the home. He and his wife (Mary Sue) have been married for over fifty years.

What have you learned and who have you learned it from? Did they say that you were meant to live a simple, quiet life? Did they say that you would never amount to anything? Did they say that you would always be a small business owner struggling to make ends meet? Even if "they" is you. Did you teach yourself this?

Well, let me tell you what an Expert says about you. He (God) says, "You are more than a conqueror, a chosen people, a royal priesthood, a holy nation, God's special possession, fearfully and wonderfully made, loved more than you will ever know. You are beautiful, unique, created for a purpose, cared for, important, strong, healed, and forgiven. You are MINE." It doesn't matter what you have learned up until now, if it doesn't line up with what God says about you, it's time to unlearn it.

Finally, Luke says that he will try to lift the spaceship from the water. Yoda tells him, "No, try not. Do, or do not, there is no try." I love this quote because if you live by this concept, then you have to go "All Out" to make sure that you get the job done. We will discuss this momentarily. The definition of try is to make an attempt. I don't like the word "try." I think that most of us use this word when we have no intention of going "All Out." So we simply try, so that we won't be held accountable in the long run.

- "I will try to hit my goals."
- "I will try to make my calls."
- "I will try to sell one hundred widgets."
- "I will try to be better than I was yesterday."
- "I will try to be a better person."

John Kizziah never paid me a dime for trying to sell a policy. No matter how hard I tried, he wouldn't budge. The monster! Let's be honest. If you're in the sales business, what do you think when a prospect says, "I'll try to come to your office next week"? You know for a fact that this person is not going to show up. There is NO commitment in the word try. Again, we use this word to make ourselves feel better if we fail (and we will fail at times), or we have no intentions on going "All Out." When I worked for John, we would have certain sales goals. If the goal was to write fifty policies, then I would say, "I'm going to write fifty policies." I never said I would try to do that.

Here's what happens most of the time when you make that type of statement. First, you spoke something positive. You said, "I can vs. I can't". Next, you have put your word out there, and your team is counting on you to do what you said that you would do. It makes you work harder, or smarter, or longer, or better, or whatever you have to do to get the job done. If the goal was one hundred and I didn't want to exert the energy and actions necessary to write one hundred policies, I would say no. I will do fifty or sixty or seventy or whatever. Whatever number I agreed to, I would bust my butt to make sure that number was met. I was the life insurance Team Leader, so I would ask my team for a definite sales goal; a number that I could count on. I did not want to hear that terrible word try (to make an attempt).

Let your yes be yes, and your no be no in business and life. If you tell a customer or especially a loved one that you will do something, then go "All Out" to make sure that you do just that. Remove the word try from your vocabulary and see how much more you will get done.

In business, and definitely in life, John Maxwell says there are four types of people: Cop Outs, Hold Outs, Drop Outs, and All Outs.

Cop Outs set no goals and make no decisions. They are happy living off the work that others do, whether it be the government or family members or friends. They have nothing and want nothing out of life unless it's free. These are the same people that believe that they are owed something from society.

They would rather have a "hand-out" than a "hand-up". No one owes any of us anything. We each are responsible for our results in life. It doesn't matter our circumstances or situations. Our situation may be more difficult than the next person's. Our beginning may have been harder than the person who was born with a "silver spoon" in their mouth, but that doesn't mean that we get to throw our hands in the air and say, "Woe is me, gimme, gimme, gimme." Decide that you want more out of life, and start working towards that new you. Life doesn't have a remote control. You have to get up and change the channel yourself. If I were a product of my circumstances, a little black boy growing up in the projects, dealing with everything that goes along with that life, I should not be writing this book. I should not be traveling around the country inspiring others to follow their dreams. Cop Outs sit back, complain and blame others for their failures.

Hold Outs, on the other hand, have beautiful goals and dreams, but they are afraid to respond to challenges. They lack the self-confidence to overcome challenges, rejection, and fear. Hold Outs do nothing to make their dreams come true. I know this one like the back of my hand because I was a Hold Out. I have been speaking, teaching and training organizations and individuals for over ten years. People would always tell me how good I was and how blessed they were after hearing my message, no matter the topic. Time and time again, I was told that I should be a motivational speaker. Deep in my heart, I wanted to do this, but I lacked the self-confidence to move forward. I dreamed of being on a large stage speaking to thousands of people, but my self-doubt told me that it would never happen. I thought that I didn't have the education, the skills, the knowledge, and whatever it might take to realize such a goal. I was simply making excuses. For ten years, I held out on my dream, ten years allowing excuses and fear to keep me bound. I have also wanted to write a book for the past five years. Again, I allowed fear and self-doubt to paralyze me. Who wants to read what I have to say? Do I have anything to say at all? For the last ten years, everyone looked at me and saw an energetic, humorous and strong Marine on the outside, but had no idea that I was dealing with insecurity on the inside. It still tries to creep in from time to time. So how did I deal with these insecurities? I began to listen to the Expert. What does God say about me? I now walk in the strength of God and His anointing.

Mark Twain said, "The two most important days in your life, are the day that you were born, and the day that you realize why." I now realize why I was born. Here is something else that the Expert says about you and me: Jerimiah 29:11 says, *"Before I formed you in the womb, I knew you; before you were born, I set you apart…For I know the plans I have for you,"* declares the LORD, *"plans to prosper you and not to harm you, plans to give you hope and a future."* God doesn't make mistakes. He has a plan for your life and your business. Seek Him diligently and He will show you, though it may be one scene at a time.

Drop Outs clearly define their goals. In the beginning they work hard to make their dreams come true, but when the going gets tough, they quit. I guess that the best definition of a Drop Out would be... a quitter. Now, don't be discouraged because the great thing about being a quitter is that you can start again. You are not dead; You simply quit. The true reason that we quit anything is that we want the easy way out. It's so much easier to walk away than to stay and work hard. The problem with quitting is that we start to build a pattern, a habit if you will. It's known as the fight or flight syndrome. When faced with adversity, we all will either fight to overcome that adversity, or run away from it. American Novelist James Baldwin says, "Not everything that is faced can be changed, but nothing can be changed until it is faced." If you allow it, life will beat you up and try to take you out. We all are hit with life circumstances. What separates the winners from the losers has to do with how we respond to those circumstances. Getting knocked down is going to happen, so we might as well prepare for it. The key is to get back up and keep fighting. Keep moving forward. Keep pursuing those goals and dreams. Fight the good fight of faith. Many of life's failures are people who did not realize how close they were to success when they gave up. Tape this on your mirror or somewhere that you will see every day: "I am allowed to scream. I am allowed to cry. I am not allowed to QUIT!"

All Outs want to shine as "inspiration" to others. Once they set a goal, they never quit. Even when the price becomes high and the challenges mount, they never quit. Their "can-do" attitude carries them to greatness. This speaks directly to what I was saying about the word "try." All Outs seldom use that word. We say things like, "I guarantee, I will, I promise, you can count on me." Sometimes we miss the mark. We fail. When we started out, failure did not enter our mind. More often than not, we don't fail because we jump over hurdles and run through obstacles, because we said that we were going to do whatever the job would take to get done. A few years ago there was a contest to see who could make the most life sales in a 60-day period. If I truly want to win at something, nothing can stop me. I believe that we all possess this inner strength. If it's important to us, we will find a way. If it's not, we will find an excuse. That's true about everything in life and business. Again, a person, who truly wants to win, first thinks about how it is possible rather than why it's not. So change your thinking and you will change your life.

Back to the story. The other teams did not know this about me. If they did, I am sure they would not have started the trash talking. Some people are motivated by inspiration while others are motivated by telling them that it can't be done. When the competition started, I went to work, making my calls as usual. I called all the contacts in my phone, asked for referrals, and asked my referrals for referrals. I went door to door in my neighborhood and my business district. I purposely wore my red work shirt to the grocery store, restaurants, and running errands so that I could approach individuals wherever I was. I remember making a five-hour round trip drive to a different city to meet a customer. I was willing to go the extra mile. I met one customer at a nightclub, and we signed the paperwork on the hood of my car. Most of my sales were made outside of my office and after working hours. I made calls and sent text messages 'til 9 p.m. and sent emails till midnight. Before I went to bed, I made a list of all the people I wanted to talk to the next day and those I needed to follow up with (the fortune is in the follow-up). The next morning, I was at it again non-stop. When the 60 days were over, I had made twice as many sales as my closest competitor.

There were lots of congratulations and lots of bragging

(none by me of course). They held a nice banquet and gave out awards. They asked me to speak to the group and tell everyone how I accomplished my task. I was excited and ready to share. Everyone sat on the edge of their seats; pen in hand ready to take notes. When I started to share what I'd done; one by one, the pens began to lie down. They sat back in their seats. Their minds began to wander, and they lost interest. They did not want to hear about the work that I'd put in. They were all looking for The Magic Pill. You see, I didn't do anything special or spectacular. Everyone sitting in that room could have done exactly what I did and achieved the same if not better results. They simply weren't willing to go All Out. They wanted a quick fix. There is no substitution for hard work. Go All Out!

Now ask yourself which one are you? Cop Out, Hold Out, Drop Out or All Out? If you don't like your answer, I've got good news. It's not too late to change.

#5 IN ORDER TO WIN IN LIFE & BUSINESS, YOU HAVE TO GO ALL OUT WHEN WORKING TOWARDS YOUR GOALS. DON'T QUIT. YOUR BREAKTHROUGH IS CLOSER THAN YOU REALIZE.

"Don't be upset by the results you didn't get from the work you didn't do."
- Unknown

"I am a great believer in luck. I find that the harder I work, the more luck I have."
- Thomas Jefferson

"10 To Win"

Notes:

CHAPTER 6

FIND A NEW ROOM

"10 To Win"

It's almost 9 a.m. when I arrive at the classroom. There are fruits, bagels, juice, water and of course coffee, sitting on the table in the rear of the class. The mood is light, and I make small talk with some of the others as more people begin to arrive. We are all top selling insurance professionals, here today for a study group, and I am eager to get started. The plan is to talk with each other, share best practices and learn from one another. What are you doing that's working? What am I doing that's working? There are approximately twenty people in the classroom as the organizer begins to speak. She gives a quick rundown of the schedule that lasts until 12 p.m. As we all begin to share our ideas and sales techniques, it is immediately evident by others in the room that I have the most to share.

Thirty minutes into the session, I am the focal point of the discussion. They ask me question after question, and I can answer each question confidently, providing them with a new sales technique that they are eager to try. By the next hour, I am now up in front of the class drawing diagrams on the board, role playing and leading the class. It now feels like I am the coach rather than a participant.

All eyes are on me, and everyone is taking notes as fast as they can. I have an answer for every objection that they can think of. I am in the zone. I am confident and a bit cocky as well. I came to participate, but now I was running the study group. I was the top salesperson in the room, and it felt good. When I finished the session, there were lots of "Thank Yous" from the participants. Everyone, including myself, was looking forward to the next study group that was to be held the next quarter. I remember coming back to the office and telling my co-workers how the day went. I also remember doing a little bragging to my wife on how the session went as well.

About a month later, I had a lunch meeting with a colleague of mine whom I'd recently met. He would later become my mentor, teacher and a good friend. His name is David Anderson, owner of Nautilus Financial. During the lunch, we started talking about sales techniques and strategies. 30 minutes into the lunch, I began to realize that I didn't

<u>David Anderson</u>
NautilusFinancialStrategies.com

Find A New Room

know as much as I thought I did about sales. An hour into the lunch, I realize that I have been going about my sales career all the wrong way. An hour later, it ended up being a three-hour lunch, I'd made up my mind that I was going to completely scrap the sales techniques I'd used before and become a student of David's "Non-Convincing Language" technique.

This technique teaches you how to have a higher closing ratio, through dialog, without having to convince your customers to buy. I've never seen anything like it before. By implementing only a fraction of this technique, I saw my closing ratio increase dramatically. I was also having more fun and experiencing less stress. I soon found that this technique can also be used when dealing with family as well. Using his technique also helped me obtain a significant contract with The Risk Advisor Institute, a training company. I now travel the country teaching insurance agents a better way to present their services to their customers.

I was the top salesperson in the first room. Everyone was hanging on my every word. I felt confident in my craft, and I had been doing a pretty good job as well. But when I met David, I quickly realized that if I wanted to become better at what I was doing, I had to find a new room. I had to surround myself with someone who could pull me up to their level of expertise and their way of thinking. There is no doubt in my mind that if I had stayed in the first room, I would not be where I am today regarding sales. I would not have grown. Yes, it felt good being looked up to. It felt good having all the right answers, but I had to grow up, to go up to the next level.

If you own a business, it is important to surround yourself with those who can help improve your business. For example, a business coach, a book on business, television shows, or other business owners who are having success. You can also pick up business tips and ideas from experts. Marcus Lemonis from CNBC's The Profit has great business fundamentals that you can learn from. A six-word statement that can destroy or keep your business stagnant is "We've always done it this way." We can never get to the point where we think that we know it all. We should all constantly find a new room in whatever area it is in which we wish to succeed.

There was once a little boy who ran home from school, eager to tell his mother about the sales contest in which the grand prize was a brand new bicycle. Whoever sold the most candy bars would be declared the winner. He finished his homework quickly and asked his mother if he could go around the neighborhood to sell his candy bars. She agreed, so off he went. He returned 30 minutes later downtrodden. When his mother asked how it went, he told her that he hadn't sold any candy bars.

She asked to hear his sales pitch. The little boy recalled what happened. I knocked on the door and said, "I'm selling candy bars for school, you don't wanna buy any, do you?" His mother consoled him and said that he should try again tomorrow. The next day, his mother coached him on what to say when he was about to go out. One hour later, the little boy returned ecstatic. He couldn't wait to tell his mother what happened. I knocked on the door and said, "I'm selling candy bars for school. I have Baby Ruth for $1 and Butterfinger for $1, *which one* would you like?" He had sold an entire box of candy bars.

The next day, he came home eager to go at it again, but his mother wanted to coach him again. The little boy was impatient and said that he didn't need any more coaching. What he did yesterday worked so why should he change anything. If it's not broken, don't fix it. His mother persisted, and the little boy reluctantly accepted the coaching. Once again, he returned an hour later, even more, excited than the day before. And once again, he couldn't wait to tell his mother what happened. I knocked on the door and said, "I'm selling candy bars for school, I have Baby Ruth for $1 and Butterfinger for $1, *how many* would you like?" He sold two boxes of candy bars in the same amount of time. Because he was willing to receive coaching, he increased his productivity in the same amount of time.

Not only will this work in a business with sales, but it

will also work in your personal life as well. I realized that if I wanted to grow in any area, all I had to do was find someone succeeding in that area and attach myself to them. I know it seems simple, but the first hurdle was realizing that I needed help.

The second hurdle was finding someone willing to help. You will be happy to know that there are plenty of people out there willing to lend a helping hand. When I wanted to become a better salesperson, I went into a room with David Anderson. When I wanted to become a better man of God, I went into a room with Rodney Stovall. When I wanted to become a better speaker, I went into a room with Bill Whitley and Mary Riesberg. When I wanted to learn how to be a better husband and father, I went into a room with Anthony McMillan. Sometimes you may have to demand help.

One day, I was sitting in my office, and Rob Hazewinkel walked in, sat down and said, "I'm here to let you know that you're my mentor now." What? I thought that the process was to ask someone to be your mentor. That wasn't Rob's process. At the time, I didn't want to be anyone's mentor, but guess what I said? Okay! It forced me to find a new room. I had to get a mentor so I would know what mentors did. I guess it worked out pretty well for both Rob and me. We became good friends. I followed my dream and started my own speaking business.

Find A New Room

As you read in chapter one, and Rob finally realized his dream when he became the owner of MaxFit in Pace, FL. By the way, it's pretty difficult to mentor someone and tell them to follow their dreams if you're not following yours. So I say, "Thank you, Rob, for forcing me to step up to the plate." I guess, sometimes you can be pushed into a new room.

The great thing about being in a new room is that not only do you learn from the individuals in that room, you actually end up being a blessing to them as well. All of us have something to offer. There is no one on this earth that has NO value. It doesn't matter how you feel about yourself, and it doesn't matter what your current circumstances may be; YOU ARE VALUABLE AND HAVE SOMETHING TO OFFER TO SOMEONE ELSE. Many times my mentors have told me that I have taught and blessed them just as much as they have taught and blessed me. Proverbs 27:17 says, *"As iron sharpens iron, so one person sharpens another."*

Famed author and motivational speaker, Jim Rohn said, "You are the average of the five people you spend the most time with." Think about that for a minute. *Stop reading and think about that.* Now write down the names of those five people. Look at their lifestyle, their attitude, their behavior and their income. Whether you like it or not, you fit somewhere right in the middle. The only way to move up the ladder of influence is to find a new room. You have to change the people with whom you spend the most time. We can't grow if we stay in the same place we were last month or last year. We can't grow if we keep associating with the same people we associated with last month or last year. I'm not saying that you have to drop your friends. I'm saying that if you want to grow, you will want to find new friends, mentors, and bring your old friends along so you can grow together.

Unfortunately, your old friends may not want to grow or go with you. They may verbally say that they do, but their actions say otherwise. Are you going to let them hold you back? Are you going to let them keep you from growing? If the answer is no, then find a new room. Those friends will end up dropping themselves voluntarily. You just keep moving forward, changing your average. Remember, sometimes we have to let go of what's killing us, even if it's killing us to let go.

Radio personality, author, and speaker, Earl Nightingale wrote a book called <u>The Strangest Secret</u>. It is a short book but one of the most influential books I have ever read. At one point in the book, he states that we are exactly where we want to be in life whether we will admit it or not. I totally agree because where we are in life and business has to do with the decisions that we have made. Most people won't agree because they blame where they are in life on their circumstances.

Find A New Room

Nobel Prize and Oscar-winning playwright, George Bernard Shaw said, "People are always blaming their circumstances for what they are. I don't believe in circumstances. The people who get on in this world are the people who get up and look for the circumstances they want, and if they can't find them, make them." Do you consider yourself a victim of circumstances? Bad things happen to us all, some, worse than others. We still have to decide on how we respond to those things. It's our choice.

There is a quote that says, "Show me your friends and I'll show you your future." Where we go in life has everything to do with who we surround ourselves with. In chapter one, I talked about surrounding yourself with those who make your baby (dream) leap. It's only pride or complacency that makes us want to stay in the same room. If you're the smartest person in the room, find a new room.

Businessman, author, and speaker, Robert Kiyosaki says that rich people surround themselves with people who are smarter than they are. Business owners hire employees who are smarter, so they can help take the company to the next level. The word "rich" can have a different meaning to different people. If you want a rich marriage, find a new room with a couple who has a rich marriage. If you want a rich relationship with your children, find a new room with a mother or father who has that relationship. Staying in the same room, surrounded by the same people will yield the same results. Albert Einstein said, "Isanity is doing the same thing over and over and expecting different results."

I have a personal story that I almost didn't put in the book. But the title of the book is How to Win in Life and Business. And my wife Erin always says, "What's from the heart touches the heart." So here it goes. At one point, Erin and I hit a rough patch in our marriage. Over the years, we've had our ups and downs but nothing of this magnitude. I couldn't put my finger on it except to say that I just didn't want to be married anymore. Of course, I came up with every excuse in the book, "We've grown apart; she doesn't understand me anymore; I would be better off by myself." You name it: I thought it.

Things became so bad that I eventually moved out. On the outside, everyone around us thought that we had the perfect marriage, and we were such a cute couple. We were leaders in the community, had wonderful kids, but we both were dying on the inside. Only those very close to us knew what was going on. It was extremely difficult on our young children as well. They didn't understand why this was happening. Of course, we started to receive all kinds of advice from those close to us, our friends and family. My very best friend talked to me often. He stated that he wanted me to be happy, and if leaving would make me happy, then that's what I should I do. He would support me either way, stay or leave. I liked that advice. It felt good to me. I was happy right where I was. I liked this room. I spent a lot of time in this room with my friend. I made up my mind that I wasn't going home. I even came up with a shared-custody plan regarding our children. Things were going to work out just fine.

My pastor, Anthony McMillan, was aware of our situation and asked to meet with me. Truth be told, I didn't want us to meet because I knew that he would try to get me to go back home. Nevertheless, I agreed to meet him. Guards up! From the very beginning, he made it clear that his only objective was to make sure that my relationship with God was where it needed to be. He also told me that any issues that I had, if I didn't address them, would be taken into my next relationship, whether it be with Erin or someone else. Wow, this was different. Other people who had advised me on the issue were adamant that I had to stay in the relationship, no matter what. Not once did he bring up my relationship with Erin; rather, we talked

Pastor Anthony & Kelly McMillan

about my relationship with God. He gave me books to read, scriptures to meditate on, and praise and worship songs to listen to. We talked on the phone and often texted, no matter how late it was. He listened, gave advice and never passed judgment. I was completely open and honest with him. I was learning how to get closer to God by being in a room with this man on a weekly basis.

By the third month, I was asking him questions about my marriage. By the fourth month, I was talking about going back home; and by the fifth month, I was willing to meet with Erin if she was open to it. And she was, because my pastor's wife, Kelly, had been meeting with Erin all along, giving her the same counseling that I had been receiving. They set us up, y'all. By month six, I was back home where I belonged. The four of us continued to meet for some time after I returned home and today, our marriage is stronger than ever. Our marriage isn't perfect, but we have both made a commitment to always keep our eyes fixed on Him (God) and not one another. You see, I was comfortable in the first room. The new room pulled me out of my comfort zone. It encouraged me to get closer to God and seek Him. Proverbs 3:5-6 says, *"Trust in the Lord with all your heart and do not depend on your understanding. But in all your ways acknowledge him, and he will direct your path."*

If I had stayed in the first room, I wouldn't have grown. I wouldn't have learned the things I needed to know to have a successful, fulfilling marriage. Keep in mind that God does not play favoritism. If He did it for my wife and me, He can surely do the same for you and your spouse. God is able.

#6 In order to Win in Life & Business, you have to find a new room. Surround yourself with people who have success in the area in which you wish to also succeed.

"You become like the 5 people you spend the most time with. Choose carefully." - Anonymous

"People inspire you, or they drain you…pick them wisely." - Hans Hansen

"10 To Win"

Notes:

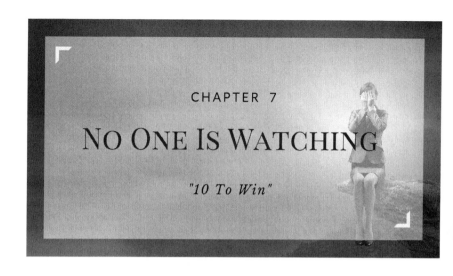

CHAPTER 7

NO ONE IS WATCHING

"10 To Win"

It was the end of the sales period, and I was behind on my sales goal. I needed to make a large life insurance sale to receive my quarterly bonus. I wasn't sure how I was going to do it, but I was sure that it was going to get done. Appointment after appointment, the customers came in; and appointment after appointment, the customers left without buying anything. I didn't understand it. I was giving it my best, but nothing was happening. I kept getting put off, "Let me think about it," or "Yes I want it, but let's wait until next month." I was extremely frustrated and to be honest, a little desperate. When you work on commission sales (If I sell, I get paid; if I don't sell, I don't get paid.), it can become stressful at times.

Although I was in charge of making my schedule, I was constantly working to keep my pipeline of prospects full. It was down to the last few days when Christopher came in. He was coming in for a "Your World" review. This is a conversation that we have with our customers in order to protect them against the seven major risks that we all face. The conversation started just like all the others had. I learned that Christopher had a wife and three children, and he was a new business owner. He had two vehicles and was a homeowner as well. He earned a moderate income, and he was the breadwinner. He and his wife had debt and little to no savings in the bank. Christopher was the typical American family. During the conversation, I discovered that because Christopher was a business owner, he had to provide benefits for himself and his family. He made sure that the health insurance for his family was taken care of. We found that he had a need for disability insurance (income replacement), retirement and life insurance. At the end of the conversation, I asked him which of these three risks was most important to him. He immediately stated that it was the life insurance. If something were to happen to him, he wanted to make sure that his family would be well taken care of.

We began to have a conversation about life insurance. I explained the difference between permanent insurance and term insurance. Permanent insurance can last a lifetime and builds cash value the longer you have it, but costs more money. Term insurance is temporary and has no cash value but costs less money. We also established a monthly amount that he could afford to pay each month for his life insurance. Right from the beginning, Christopher wanted nothing to do with term insurance. I explained that because of the cost of permanent insurance, he would not be able to purchase much insurance. He said that he understood but still wanted the permanent. This seemed to be going my way because I would earn more from the sale of a permanent policy. I would make my sales goal for the quarter with this purchase. I did my job, right? I explained the difference, and he still wanted to buy the permanent insurance. This was a perfectly legal sale.

Here's the problem. If Christopher had purchased this policy and something happened to him, his wife would not have enough life insurance to pay off the house, send the kids to college or have a continuing monthly income to support the family. The term policy would have been able to do these things for Christopher's family. I took the time to explain this to him. He understood, agreed and purchased the term policy. He stood up, shook my hand and thanked me. When Chris left my office, I felt good about my decision. I knew that I'd done the right thing, even though no one was watching.

I missed part of my bonus that quarter, but I didn't regret my decision one bit. I have taken short cuts in the past as a young man, and I was not going back down that road again. Remember, trust takes years to build, seconds to break and forever to repair. Christopher appreciated my honesty and direction. He said that I was "looking out for him and his family." He later introduced me to another business owner who purchased other policies with me. Your reputation follows you, no matter what that reputation may be.

This chapter, "No One Is Watching", deals with our integrity. Some would refer to it as our character; although, a lot of different aspects make up one's character. The official definition of integrity is, "The quality of being honest and having strong moral principles." But I once heard someone describe it simply as, "What you do when no one is watching." When no one is watching, will you be honest? When no one is watching, do you have strong moral principles? Are you willing to compromise your integrity to make $1?" You say no. What about $1,000,000? Ask yourself, "What's my integrity worth?" We would all like to think that we would do the right thing. I'm sure that most of us would, but we never really know until we are faced with a situation. That's when your true character comes out.

Take a look at this list of professions on the next page. It shows certain professions and the *public trust* that we have for each profession. Some may shock you, while others I am sure will not. You may even agree.

Firemen	40%	Military	38%
Medical	25%	Police	14%
Lawyers	5%	Car Salesmen	2%
Insurance	2%	Politicians	1%

Now whether you agree or disagree with this list, according to my extensive research (Google search), that is how the chips fall.

My wife works for a well-known financial company. When she was hired, they sent her to a diversity class. In one of the exercises, they had to write down stereotypes of other races and genders. She stated that it was a sad but eye-opening experience of how we view each other. The class was designed to put stereotypes to rest while acknowledging them, regardless if they were true or not. It's how people see your profession, and you may be the only person who can change that impression. If I asked you to write down three words to describe a lawyer, what would those words be? Honest? Forthcoming? Sincere? What if I asked you to describe a politician? Truthful? Straightforward? Authentic?

The sad truth is that these are not words that the average person would use to describe these professions. But I know lawyers and politicians whom you could use these words to describe today. If someone mentions the name of your business, what comes to people's mind? Does your business have a reputation for being fair and honest, or taking advantage of customers? Do you even care about the public perception of your business? Do you have employees that represent your business with integrity? Keep this in mind. Most employees deal with customers the way they see their employers deal with customers - fair and honest, or crooked and dishonest. It's your business and your reputation.

Let's talk briefly about integrity in the home. How do your family members view you? How is your character when it comes to your loved ones? Believe it or not, there was a time that I didn't think that I had to have integrity when it came to dealing with my kids. I thought that it was okay to go back on my word regarding them. I soon discovered that this should not be the case when, one day, my youngest son Josiah said to me, "Dad, you never tell the truth." I was schocked. What did he mean? I am a man of integrity. Just ask anyone. Furious, I asked what he was referring to? He said, "You always say that you are going to take us to the toy store, but you never do. You say that you will watch a show with us, but you never do. You say that you will be home before we go to bed, but we don't see you until the next morning." I could not argue with my son. Josiah was right.

The small things, or things that I considered to be small,

were proving me to be a man who did not keep his word with his kids. Let's remember that integrity starts at home. You should be a person of our word, especially when it comes to those precious, little souls, in our family, who look up to us and internalize every word you speak to them. Our family should be able to count on our word, just like we can count on God's word. Mark 13:31 says, *"Heaven and earth will pass away, but my words will never pass away."* Don't let your words pass away when dealing with others.

"He is so good at sales, that he could sell ice to Eskimos." This quote has always been meant as a compliment. Being one of the top insurance salesmen in my area, I used to accept this as a compliment. But speaker, author and my good friend, Bill Whitley says that his couldn't be further from the truth. Think about it. If you are selling ice to an Eskimo, then you are selling them something that they don't need. Where is the integrity in that? This is the reason that insurance professionals have the stereotype that we have today is from selling customers things

that they don't need. The Eskimo will never say "thank-you" for the ice. They will never introduce you to their Eskimo friends.

I didn't sell ice to Christopher. He thanked me, and he sent me more referrals and more business. Making a quick sale is not worth damaging the reputation of your business.

So, from now on, if someone uses that quote to describe you, be quick to explain to them the difference. We do what's right for our customers. Incidentally, Bill has started the "No Ice For Eskimos" movement. Contact him at www.RiskAdvisorInstitute.com to purchase your desk top sign. It will have your customers asking questions.

When I was a young Lance Corporal (E-3) in the Marine Corps, I had the opportunity to be selected for a Meritorious Promotion. This meant that I would compete for the rank of Corporal (E-4) against ten to twelve other top Lance Corporals within my battalion and possibly be promoted early. This was a very big deal. I would stand at attention before a board (panel), comprised of eight First Sergeants (E-8) and Sergeant Majors (E-9), over one hundred fifty years of military experience between them, and answer approximately twenty to twenty five questions concerning the Marine Corps. Here's the problem, the questions could be anything from the two hundred plus years the Marine Corps has been in existence, so I had to study everything. Imagine the interview from hell, multiply it by three, and you still wouldn't understand. One of the things that I made sure to memorize was the fourteen Marine

<u>Marine Corps Corporal Insignia</u>

Corps Leadership Traits. If I were going to be a leader, I had better know these traits. We used an acronym to help us remember.

JJ DID TIE BUCKLE

Justice: Am I for what's right?
Judgment: Do I make good decisions?
Decisiveness: Do I make decisions quickly and effectively?
Initiative: Do I act without being told to do so?
Dependability: Can others count on me?
Tact: Do I utilize understanding when dealing with others?
Integrity: What do I do when no one is watching?
Enthusiasm: Am I eager and excited about my business/life?
Bearing: How do I carry myself around others?
Unselfishness: Do I show concern for others before myself?
Courage: Am I doing what needs to be done even though I'm afraid?
Knowledge: Am I studying my craft to become better?
Loyalty: Do I show strong support or allegiance to others?
Endurance: Am I moving forward even though my body says I can't?

The Marine Corps constantly stressed these important leadership traits because every Marine should be a leader. We were all constantly being judged by our peers and superiors by these fourteen traits. During our quarterly evals (evaluations), this is how we received our proficiency and conduct grades. The one leadership trait that was stressed above all the others was integrity. None of the other thirteen mean anything unless a Marine has integrity. If a Marine says he's going to do something, he does it. A Marine does not dishonor himself, his unit, The Corps or his country. A Marine does the right thing when no one is watching. Once a Marine, always a Marine.

Now don't tell my kids this, but Marines are human. I have them convinced otherwise. Sometimes we all miss the mark, and we all get it wrong at times. I believe what the Marine Corps believes. It does not matter how great your business is, or how good of a leader you are, or how nice you are, or how much money you have, or your status in the community. If you are not a person of integrity, if your character is not beyond reproach, then it's all for nothing. Matthew 7:15 says, *"They come to you in sheep's clothing, but inwardly they are ferocious wolves. By their fruit you will recognize them."*

By the way, in case you were wondering, I blew the competition away and was promoted to Corporal (Meritoriously) in The United States Marine Corps, to rank as such from the second day of December, in the year of our Lord nineteen hundred eighty-nine.

#7 In order to Win in Life & Business, you must do what's right even when no one is watching.

"Character is much easier kept than recovered." - Thomas Paine

"People may doubt what you say. But they will always believe what you do."

"10 To Win"

Notes:

CHAPTER 8
GOLD VS PLATINUM
"10 To Win"

I met my good friend Kirk Waters for our monthly lunch. We chose a different location each time, and we loved to catch up on family, work, and life in general. On this particular day, we met at a local restaurant in East Pensacola (They have the best mushroom soup.) It was a bit crowded because of the lunch time rush, but the owner greeted us with a smile as she led us to our seats. As we sat there briefly making small talk, our server approached us, notepad in hand, ready to take our order. She had a slender build, blonde hair, glasses and was in her mid-thirties. She had a half-smile on her face and was pleasant in her greeting to us, but I could tell that she was forcing her pleasantries because it was the right thing to do. She introduced herself as Joelle as she asked us for our drink orders.

It was an average day, and Joelle appeared to be the average server except for one thing. Joelle was wearing a button that read, "Please make me feel good about myself." I was astonished. I couldn't believe it. Why would someone wear such a button? I was tempted to ask her about the button, but I didn't want to embarrass her. Was this some kind of a joke? Were we on some type of hidden camera show? Kirk and I simply looked at each other in amazement as we gave Joelle our drink orders. When she left the table, we discussed this button. Is this for real? Should we say something? Why is it our job to make her feel good about herself? We were there to be served, and besides that, I've got my own problems that I'm dealing with right now. Nevertheless, we decided that if someone was bold enough to wear a button like that, then they must be desperate. I guess we never know what others are going through sometimes until it's too late.

So Kirk and I figured that we would do our best to make sure that Joelle felt good about herself before we left the restaurant. When she returned with our drinks and asked to take our order, I said, "First tell us how you are doing today, Joelle?" She paused for a second. We could tell that she was taken off guard. Maybe everyone else had ignored her button. She smiled, said that she was doing fine, and thanked me for asking. As I gave her my order, cobb salad extra shrimp, Kirk asked, "Joelle, what do you recommend?" Joelle told him about some of the favorite items on the menu. Kirk chose one and responded, "Thank you, Joelle. I appreciate that." Joelle responded, "My pleasure" and was off to fulfill our order. We could immediately see that the half-smile she initially had now turned to a full sincere smile. Ironically, Kirk and I were now smiling, and we felt pretty good about putting a smile on Joelle's face. But there was more work to do.

Kirk and I continued with our conversation until Joelle returned with our meals. Rather than ignoring her and barking out orders (more tea, more napkins, ketchup, etc.), we looked Joelle in the eye, smiled, showed our appreciation and thanked her for our meals. Again, she smiled and asked if there was anything that we needed. Then we asked for what we needed. Joelle would return to our table from time to time just to make sure that we didn't need anything else. We would always stop talking, look Joelle in the eye, smile and say, "No thank you." We would also comment to her on how good the food tasted.

I must admit that in the past I would often wave my hand at the server as if trying to shoo away a fly. We finished our meals and Joelle brought us our ticket. I had to pay for both meals because Kirk had conveniently forgotten his wallet. Before she left our table, I said to her, "Joelle, I eat out quite often, and this has been one of the most pleasant dining experiences I have ever had. Thank You so much." Joelle put her hand over her heart and said, "Aww, thank you so much. You have made my day." "No, Joelle, you've made my day," I replied. Kirk joined in with compliments about her attention to detail, her pleasant smile, and her food recommendation was on point. As she walked away, Kirk and I could see that she now had a life-sized smile on her face. Of course, I left her a nice tip, while Kirk left a written note on the receipt, "Best service ever." Joelle was extremely appreciative of our kindness, and she made it known to us before we left. Kirk and I stood outside and talked for a minute.

How fascinating it was that someone who needed that attention had the courage to ask for it. Who knows, we may have saved that young woman's life that day. We never really know what the person to the left of us and the right of us are going through unless they choose to share with us. As Kirk and I went on our way, I felt fulfilled and rewarded. It's amazing how doing something nice for someone else can have this effect on you. I love it!

OK, if you haven't figured it out by now, you should know that Joelle wasn't wearing a "Please make me feel good about myself" button. At least, she wasn't wearing one on the outside. But I can promise you that many of us wear these buttons on the inside. There are people around us on a daily basis just begging to be healed of hurt, depression, sorrow and many other symptoms that sometimes can't be seen by the naked eye.

I was reminded of this when a friend of mine took his life. We'd just had lunch together at this same restaurant, and we were scheduled to attend an event together just days after this tragedy. I often still ask myself if there was something that I could have said, or done differently, or maybe I missed something. Was he wearing a button and I missed it because I was so caught up in my problems? It bothered me for days. All any of us can do is treat the people around us with love and respect. Slow down and take the time to tell them that we appreciate them. No matter who the person may be--for example, a loved one, an employee or a stranger. We all need to hear those words every once in a while: I appreciate you.

I attended a Mastermind Pensacola meeting. During the presentation, the organizer, Ron Spradling asked everyone to take out their cell phone and text three people, three simple words, "I appreciate you." He then asked that we share some of the responses throughout the meeting. You would be surprised at some of the responses. "Thank you, I needed to hear that today," "Thank you for noticing," "I appreciate you too, sorry about our fight," "You made my day," and one of my personal favorites, "What did you do now?" LOL.

It just goes to show that none of us are used to hearing

that we are appreciated. That's why it's so important to make sure that we treat those around us very well. Even if we have to imagine that they're wearing a button that says, "Please make me feel good about myself." It may sound silly, but I dare you to try it just once. Get your friends and family in on it as well. Pick someone and make them feel good about themselves today. It's a win-win situation. You think that they will be the beneficiary, but you will actually benefit from it as well.

As a matter of fact, stop reading this book right now and text three people those three simple words, "I appreciate you." Let's see what type of responses you will receive. Let's see who needed to hear from you at this very moment. Who does God bring to your mind? Listen. Text them now, right now! Don't hesitate, don't elaborate, and don't add to it, just three words. Remember, the power of life and death is in the tongue. Speak Life to someone at this very moment. You could save a life.

I titled this chapter "Gold vs. Platinum" because I was referring to The Golden Rule vs. The Platinum Rule. Amazingly, when I presented this topic at a seminar and asked the audience if they were familiar with the Platinum Rule, only one person knew what it meant. So, let's just take a moment to discuss these rules.

First, I would be remiss if I didn't mention my buddy Eddie Hill, who jokingly told us about the Aluminum Rule, which is, "Do unto others as they have done unto you." Now on the surface, this would seem like a pretty good rule. Treat people how they have treated you; for instance, an eye for an eye, right? I must admit that I struggle with the Aluminum Rule at times. It's just natural to deal people the cards that they dealt you. It's easy to do, and we justify in our minds that it's justice. They are getting what they deserved. Man, I am so glad that God does not operate through the Aluminum Rule. I'm so glad that He does not give me what I deserve.

What about you? Does God give you what you deserve? Or does He give you grace? Does He give you blessings? Does He give you chance after chance, time and time again? If you serve the same God that I serve, then I already know the answer.

I'm not saying that it's easy to treat others well when they have mistreated you. But that's where your blessings comes from. Matthew 5:43-46 says, *"You have heard that it was said, 'You shall love your neighbor and hate your enemy. But I say to you, love your enemies and pray for those who persecute you. For if you only love those who love you, what reward do you have?"* Sometimes we are wronged by family members, friends, co-workers, and employers. We want to hold a grudge against them, and no one would think us wrong for doing so, but as you can see, "What reward do you have?" Holding unforgiveness against others postpones your blessings. So "Let go and let God." Yes, that's correct. Let go and Let God. It means to let go of all unforgiveness, all your worries and all your cares and all your problems, and let God deal with them. So the next time that you feel like worrying about something, or someone wronged you and you want revenge, let go and let God.

The Golden Rule is a pretty popular rule, and everyone knows it. We learned it in elementary school. Do unto others as you would have them do unto you. Treat others as you want to be treated. Let me tell you the problem with writing a book like this. The problem is that your wife reminds you of what you wrote when you go off track. In other words, practice what you preach. Man, I love that woman. I may not like to hear what she has to say at times, but I love her. I especially love the God inside of her.

One day, my computer developed some problems, and I had to call tech support for help. I paid extra money for the protection plan. For some reason, my work e-mail would not send/receive e-mails. My personal e-mail was working just fine. I called tech support and explained the situation. The tech logged into my account and had full access to my computer and screen. It was weird seeing someone else moving my mouse around.

After about an hour on the phone and on my computer, they logged out, as they were unable to help, and suggested that I take it back to the store where I purchased it. Hmmm, I paid the bill for tech support, yet they couldn't help. Did I waste my money? Now, I started working on my PC. I wanted to send an e-mail from my personal e-mail account, but it couldn't send/receive anything. Are you kidding me? I couldn't believe this. I immediately called the tech support on the phone. Of course, I had a different operator this time, and had to explain everything all over again. His response floored me. "Sir, we don't service personal e-mail accounts, we only service work e-mail accounts." What? I was furious! When I initially called, I had one broken e-mail. I called tech support for help, they didn't help, and now I had two broken e-mails. No matter what I said, he was firm that he couldn't help me. This went on, back and forth, for about 15 minutes. I started yelling at the poor guy on the other end who remained calm and professional the entire time. I didn't use any abusive, four-letter words; though, I sure wanted to. They broke my personal email, and now it couldn't be fixed.

No email? Life as I knew it was over. Right? At least, my cell phone wasn't broken; I would have blown a head gasket. No cell phone? Why even continue living? Right? We get so attached to these gadgets that they begin to run and rule our lives. Anyway, back to the story. My wife Erin came into the room to see what led to all the yelling. She calmly reached her hand out for my cell phone. She got on the phone, explained the situation in a calm manner, apologized to the gentleman, and within the hour, they (my wife and tech support) had my personal email working again. She had this look on her face as if to say, "Really, was it that serious?" Rather than agreeing, I tried to justify my actions by saying that it was their fault. Regardless of their actions, was I demonstrating the Golden Rule? Was I treating him the way that I want to be treated? The tech support guy demonstrated the Golden Rule. My wife demonstrated the Golden Rule. But Steve Wilmer, the motivational speaker, the author, was applying the Aluminum Rule.

Matthew 5:16 says, *"Let your light shine before others, that they may see your good deeds and glorify your Father in heaven."* As I look back on this situation, I am not proud at all of the way I behaved. I was not bringing glory to God. It's been said that life is only 1% of what happens to us and 99% of how we respond to it. How do you respond to life, your family, your employees, and your customers? Let's begin to treat others with the love and respect that we would want to receive ourselves. I didn't say that it was going to be easy. Great things rarely come to us easily. We normally have to work to receive great things.

Gold vs. Platinum

Don't let someone else's actions dictate your response. Our response should always be to let our light shine and bring glory to God.

So let's talk about this mysterious Platinum Rule. The first time that I heard of this rule was from Business Network International (BNI). The Platinum Rule states you should treat others how they want to be treated. Business owners should especially take notice of the Platinum Rule. It means, treat your customers how they want to be treated, and not how you want to treat them. It's all about what your customers expect rather than what you expect from them. The Platinum Rule takes extra effort and goes the extra mile because now you are going beyond what you want and giving others what they want. If you thought that the Golden Rule was hard, you might as well skip to the next chapter because this rule is going to pull you out of your comfort zone. But you will be happy to know that everything that you want in life and business is just outside your comfort zone.

Talk with your customers, give them feedback forms, listen and find out what they want from your business. How do they want to do business with you? For years, our insurance company prided ourselves on the fact that we had local agents in the neighborhood so that you could walk right in. But then we began to listen to our customers. Now, not only can you walk in, you can call in 24hrs a day, you can conduct business online, and now there is an app that you can download and install on your smartphone so you can view all your policies. We should make every effort to cater to our customers' needs. No more business as usual. That's the Platinum Rule.

Of course, the Platinum rule can be, and should be, used in your marriage/relationship as well. The best way that I can think to describe the Platinum Rule in a relationship is to refer to the book <u>The Five Love Languages</u> by Gary Chapman that I mentioned earlier. Applying the Aluminum Rule will never give you a good relationship. "Tit-for-tat" doesn't work. "She did this, so now I'm going to do that" will fill your relationship with bitterness, anger and unforgiveness. I've tried it the Aluminum way. As noble as it may sound, even the Golden Rule will not work if you try to apply it to a relationship.

Treating your partner how you want to be treated can lead to the other person feeling unfulfilled and sometimes even unloved. Let me give you an example. The way that I show my love is doing things for people. So to show my love for my wife, I would wash and dry the clothes, do some cleaning around the house, iron the clothes, run errands, basically doing whatever needed to be done. But I thought that my wife did not love me.

She rarely offered to do any of these things for me.

My wife's way of showing love is always touching me. She would always want to hold my hand, or lay in my lap while I watch sports, or have me scratch her head until she falls asleep. Every time I walked by, she would want a kiss. She wanted me to touch her in any way possible. But she thought that I did not love her. I rarely wanted to hold hands or give hugs and kisses. We didn't understand what the problem was. We were treating each other how we wanted to be treated. I wanted her to do things for me, so I did things for her. She wanted me to touch her, so she always touched me. We were practicing the Golden Rule.

Remember, the Platinum Rule says to treat others how they want to be treated. After reading the book, Erin discovered that my love language was Acts of Service. I discovered that her love language was Physical Touch. For my wife to feel loved, I must touch her in some way. It doesn't matter to her if I clean the entire house from top to bottom. If I'm not touching her, she doesn't feel loved, and her "love tank" is empty. For me to feel loved, she must do things for me. It doesn't matter to me if she holds my hand from here to eternity. If she's not doing something for me, I don't feel loved, and my "love tank" is empty. You see, we did love each other all along. We simply did not know the proper way to communicate that love to one another. Now, I scratch her head until she falls asleep, and she takes care of the little things that I need to get done from time to time.

Wow…we do love each other. Gold vs. Platinum? Platinum wins every time. Incidentally, the five love languages are Acts of Service, Physical Touch, Quality Time, Words of Affirmation, and Gifts.

I will leave you with this. Author, poet, and civil rights activist, Dr. Maya Angelou, said, "I've learned that people will forget what you said, people will forget what you did, but people will never forget how you made them feel." The server, Joelle may forget what Kirk and I said to her, but she will never forget how we made her feel that day. The tech that I spoke to over the phone may forget my harsh words, but he'll never forget how I made him feel.

How do you treat others around you? How do you make your employees feel? How do you make your customers feel? Most importantly, how do you make your family feel? These are not questions that you are qualified to answer. Ask those around you, listen objectively, and be ready to make a change if necessary. Often, how we see ourselves is not how others see us. Some people brighten a room when they enter it; others brighten it when they leave. Which are you? If you don't like the answer, I've got good news for you. There's still time to change.

#8 IN ORDER TO WIN IN LIFE & BUSINESS, YOU HAVE TO TREAT PEOPLE WELL. PEOPLE WILL ALWAYS REMEMBER HOW YOU MADE THEM FEEL.

"Treat people like they make a difference, and they will."
- Jim Goodnight

"Be sure to taste your words before you spit them out." - Anonymous

"10 To Win"

Notes:

CHAPTER 9

JUMP!

"10 To Win"

The year was 1988. I was a young Marine Corps Infantryman. At the time, we were training in Pohang, Korea. We were training with the Korean ROK Marines. I remember they were small in stature, but very tough and disciplined. Their commander would give orders and then hit them with a stick if he felt that they didn't move quickly enough. They ran everywhere they went, and they always seemed very motivated.

Although there was a language barrier between us, we were able to communicate and understand each other just fine, with gestures and broken English. We shared food (They loved our MRE's, but their "kimchi" took some getting used to.), and even enjoyed some laughter together at times. I admired these natives. The ironic thing is that my sergeant told me that they admired us because we were US Marines. Our history has shown us to be tough, a force to be reckoned with. Now, whether he was telling the truth or not, I wasn't sure, but that statement stuck with me the entire time we were training together.

One day, it came time to do our rappel training—jumping from a high altitude while attached to a rope—at our camp. I am not afraid of heights, but if it's all the same to you, I'd rather stay on solid ground. We climbed a huge mountain that had to be the highest mountain that I've ever been on. We walked up a dirt-stricken path, that seemed to never end, that led to an opening at the top. What I saw next made my heart drop.

There was a bridge made of rope from the top of this mountain strung across to the top of a nearby mountain just as high. There was a Korean ROK Marine standing on the rope bridge half way across with a huge smile on his face. As I looked down from the mountain top, I remember thinking within me, "I could die today." There was nothing below except rocks. It was indeed a scary sight to a young man just coming into the Marine Corps!

Rope Bridge Rappel

I was not the first in line, so I had a chance to either build up the courage or fake an injury. Unfortunately, going back down the mountain was not an option. The one thing that kept running through my mind was that the native ROK Marines looked up to us, and I did not want to embarrass my platoon or the US Marine Corps in general.

My buddy Bernard Donnell was first in line. He put on a harness and walked slowly out onto the bridge. It swayed up and down with each step and made loud cracking noises as he walked closer and closer to the ROK Marine standing in the middle. The ROK Marine said something to Donnell in Korean. And just like that, Donnell jumped. The bridge shook violently up and down as Donnell let out a loud "Marine Corps" yell as he rappelled to the ground. It seemed like forever before he reached the bottom. I was about 5th in line, so I was fortunate (or unfortunate) enough to see this happen a few more times before it was my turn to dare this seemingly deadly task.

I was extremely afraid. So I tried to pump myself up with "self-talk". I kept saying over and over again, "I'm not afraid! I'm not afraid!" But it seemed my heart would jump out of my chest as it was beating so fast, and I was very nervous. That voice inside my head kept saying, "Oh yes, you are afraid." I was arguing with myself at one point—"Yes you are!" "No, I'm not!" "Yes, you are!" "No, I'm not!" The voice finally won. Yep, I was afraid.

Nevertheless, I quoted a very popular scripture to myself. 2 Timothy 1:7 says, *"God has not given us a spirit of fear, but of power, love, and a sound mind",* and I quoted it over and over. Although I believed it, I still could not stop myself from being afraid. I was confessing one thing with my mouth, but my body was not buying it. My mouth was dry, and my palms were sweaty. All my fight within was useless.

Finally, it was my turn, so here is what I did. I accepted the fear. I embraced the fear. I said, "Yes, I am afraid. I am terrified. But that's not going to stop me from jumping off this bridge." Once I accepted the fear, it no longer had power over me. I didn't pretend that it wasn't there. I acknowledged its presence and said, "I don't care that you're here; I'm moving forward anyway. I will not allow you to keep me from doing what needs to be done."

I moved forward onto the bridge, heart still pounding. The ROK Marine smiled at me and said something in Korean. There were about thirty feet of slack in the rope that was attached to me which meant that there would be a thirty-foot free fall before the rope caught. I looked down one last time (why in the world did I do that), held on tight, yelled "Wilmer on Rappel" and then jumped off the bridge...

Guess what? It was nowhere near as bad as I imagined it would be. As a matter of fact, once I jumped, it was fun. I gave out a loud "Marine Corps" yell as I rappelled down to the ground. Over and over again that day, I made that jump, and I've made that jump from different heights and different places during my time in the Marine Corps. Make no mistake about it. Each and every time I did, fear was present. I always acknowledged the fear was there, but I moved forward in spite of this. It's important to note that I did not say that I conquered fear. I said that I moved forward despite the fear. There is a big difference. I was still afraid, but I did not allow fear to stop me.

The result then and now and every time since is that it's not as bad as I thought it would be. To this day, in a lot of things that I do, fear is still present looking over my shoulder—it was even there at the time of writing this book. However, since you are reading the book (thank you), it is obvious I moved forward once again in spite of fear, and you should not allow fear to stop you either.

Whatever it is that you want to do, whatever it is that you need to do, I say, "Do it!" Yes, of course, the situation may be difficult. You may not know the outcome. You may be laughed at and even ridiculed, but "Jump". Someone once said, "If you never want to be afraid or embarrassed, then say nothing, do nothing, be nothing."

Fear is a very real emotion. I would not recommend trying to conquer fear; rather, acknowledge it and you take away its power. Everyone talks about having courage. Well, I have news for you, my friend. Contrary to popular beliefs, courage is not the absence of fear. It's moving forward even though you're afraid. Think about it, if you weren't afraid, you wouldn't need courage. You would just do it. It doesn't take courage to do the easy things. It takes courage to do the things that are most difficult for us to do.

Remember Earl Nightingale's quote? "We are where we want to be in life, whether we will admit it or not." I believe that to be true in a society like America where you have every opportunity to succeed. So what's stopping you? Take a guess.

Why haven't you started that business? **FEAR.**
Why aren't you following your passion? **FEAR.**
Why are you still at that dead-end job? **FEAR.**
Why are you still in that relationship that's tearing you down? **FEAR.**
Why haven't you addressed that situation that needs to be addressed? **FEAR.**
Why haven't you applied for that position, sung that song, written that book, made that trip or even asked that special person out to dinner? **It's nothing but FEAR!**

Fear makes us take a step backward rather than forward. It keeps us in bondage and holds back our blessings. I know this all too well because it was nothing but fear that kept me from pursuing my passion to be a professional speaker for all these years.

One of my favorite definitions for fear is False Evidence Appearing Real. Fear will lie to us. It tells us that things will be worse than they actually will be. Don't listen to it. There is a whole new world out there just waiting for you, a whole new experience and possibly a whole new life. What would you do if you knew you couldn't fail? Now ask yourself, why am I not doing it? Do I need to tell you the answer? It's just because you are afraid to "JUMP".

Have you ever seen an elephant with a rope tied around its leg, attached to a stake in the ground? Does the elephant see the rope as something he cannot escape? The answer is, yes. In this case, I see False Evidence Appearing Real to this animal. This adult elephant is more powerful than the rope that's holding him to the stake. But because of fear, he won't even try to break loose. His instinct has been conditioned from the time of birth that he can't do it. So, although he is powerful beyond measure, he allows fear to keep him bound where he is.

As humans, we are no different. When I was a young police officer with the Pensacola Police Department, I specifically remember being dispatched to a "house alarm" call. The house was located in a middle-class neighborhood. Upon my arrival, I discovered that the homeowner tripped the alarm accidently. He invited me in to look around to make sure that everything was okay. As I was inside, I remember thinking, "I will never own a home like this." At the time, I was living in a rented apartment, and home-ownership had never even crossed my mind.

I was raised in low-income housing, and then my mother moved us to the Aragon Court projects. My mother never owned a home, so I thought that I would never own a home. My grandmother never owned a home. So, my mother probably thought that she would never own a home, and the cycle continued down the line in the genealogy. Unconsciously, I put those limitations on myself. I allowed my past experiences and circumstances to dictate my future. I felt that I couldn't have it, as I felt that I didn't belong to the class of homeowners. I felt that I couldn't do it, so I never tried it at all. I allowed this False Evidence Appearing Real to stop me from daring it.

Years later after my wife Erin and I met and were married, she wanted us to buy a home of our own. I remember telling her that we couldn't. When she asked why, I had no answer. I had a lot of excuses, but no real answers. Thankfully, Erin wouldn't accept any of my excuses, and we "JUMPED" and purchased our first home. Of course, it was nowhere near as difficult as I thought it would be. It was all in my head. It was a very nice two-story home in a great subdivision. I couldn't believe that I could become a homeowner. We even went on to purchase two more homes and rental property since then. I'm now teaching my kids the benefits of being a homeowner compared to renting options.

We so often place our "inability to move forward" on our experiences, situations, and circumstances. But you are in control of your situation. Everything you want in life is on the other side of fear. So if you are dealing with fear, stop reading now, get up and draw a line on the ground or in the sand or on a piece of paper. On one side of the line, write the word "FEAR." You can see it there on the ground. Correct? It's real. It's not a figment of your imagination, is it? You wrote it. Now reach down and touch it. It is real. Now "JUMP" on the other side of that line, leaving fear behind you. It may sound crazy but do it right now—no more wasting time and no more procrastinating. This will literally give you a mental picture of what you should do the next time fear tries to stop you from moving forward. Do it!

There is a champion on the inside of each and every one of us (YES…including you) just waiting to be released, just waiting to fulfill those dreams we thought about since we were children. We were all created for success, but this world is trying to redesign us for failure. Don't allow it. Stand up and take your rightful place of authority. Be confident. Be bold. Speak back to fear and tell fear that it no longer has power over you. You will no longer conform to fear or allow it to shape your future. You are in control of your destiny. God has HUGE plans for your life, and only YOU can stop or delay those plans. No one else has that power but you.

Remember, the two most important days in your life are the day that you were born and the day that you realize why. Once you realize why, you will be unstoppable. You will be on fire and fulfilling those lifelong dreams. Yes, fear will still be an ever-present foe, but there's good news. The good news is that the battle has already been won, and you have the victory—you are an overcomer. So from this day forward, begin to walk in your victory. Feel the fear and do it anyway.

Veterans Memorial Park Pensacola, FL

#9 In order to Win in Life & Business you have to jump. Don't allow fear to hold you back or hold you down.

"The only reason why you're staying where you are instead of doing what really makes you happy is because you're afraid."
- Anonymous

Notes:

"Our deepest fear is not that we are inadequate. Our deepest fear is that we are powerful beyond measure. It is our light, not our darkness that most frightens us. We ask ourselves, who am I to be brilliant, gorgeous, talented, and fabulous? Actually, who are you not to be? You are a child of God. Your playing small does not serve the world. There is nothing enlightened about shrinking so that other people won't feel insecure around you. We are all meant to shine, as children do. We were born to make manifest the glory of God that is within us. It's not just in some of us; it's in everyone. And as we let our light shine, we unconsciously give other people permission to do the same. As we are liberated from our fear, our presence automatically liberates others."

- Marianne Williamson

CHAPTER 10
THE MAIN THING

"10 To Win"

I'd just gotten a call from Bill Whitley asking me if I was available to speak in Dodge City Kansas in two weeks. "Are you kidding me? Yes," I responded immediately. Becoming a professional speaker has been my dream for a very long time. I was excited. I immediately began preparing for this big opportunity. There was so much to do in such a short period of time. I began working on what I was going to say to my audience. This was going to be my first paid speaking engagement, and things had to run smoothly.

As I began to prepare my seminar, my oldest son Judah interrupted and wanted us to go outside and play catch. I told him about my opportunity, and he was extremely happy for me. He always supports me. He understood that I didn't have time because I was working to finish my presentation. I worked vigorously every evening preparing for my talk. The time came for me to leave for Kansas, and I was making last minute preparations and packing because I had to leave early in the morning. Judah finished his homework and wanted me to throw a few baseballs to him. I told him I wished that I could, but I had to put the finishing touches on my presentation, and I just didn't have the time that evening. I apologized, and Judah understood. He was happy that I was about to travel to Kansas. I told him that I would make sure to bring him back something. He smiled and said, "Thanks, dad."

The next day came, and I was off to Kansas. I was extremely nervous and wasn't sure what to expect. I'd dreamed about this moment for a long time, and it was finally here. This was my first time in Kansas, and I was also excited seeing Dodge City as I am a Wyatt Earp fan. I arrived in Dodge, and I met Bill at the convention center. He was to speak first, and I was to follow. He has been doing this for some time now, and he was flawless. He finished speaking and then introduced me to the audience.

This was it, my moment to sink or swim. Well, I swam, and it went extremely well. Everyone was sitting on the edge of their seats listening to me. I was in the zone. When I got off stage, there were handshakes, smiles, and congratulations. This was a two-day event, and I was sure that the second day would go just as well. I was wrong.

The second day was even better. I remember one young lady crying when I finished. She said that I had inspired her to do what she knew needed to be done. God was moving during my presentation. After everyone had gone, Bill told me that he was extremely happy with my presentation. As a matter of fact, he was very much impressed; he invited me to travel to North Carolina with him in three weeks to do the same presentation again. I couldn't believe this was happening. I flew home the next day, with gifts for the family, anxious to tell everyone how it went. Erin and the kids were ecstatic at my report. I gave them a play-by-play account of how the seminar went. I also told them about the upcoming event that Bill wanted me to attend.

I was home, but I had to prepare for my next event. Judah was especially proud of me. He is always trying to impress dad. He just wants me to be proud of him, and of course, I am. He asked me to go outside and play catch with him, but I was a little tired from traveling. I promised that I would play catch the next day. Judah always understood. We awoke early the next day to head to the ball field for Judah's baseball game. I told a few of the dads about my trip to Kansas. There were congratulations and "Atta boys" from everyone. I have to admit, it felt very good. I settled in to watch the kids play ball. It was a very good game and a close game as well. Judah was playing left field, and not getting a lot of balls I might add. The next kid came up to bat and hit a "pop fly" to the left field. Judah was in good position underneath the ball. As the ball came down, it missed his glove and hit the ground. Judah immediately picked it up and made the throw to third base, but the runner on second had already scored. I saw that Judah was disappointed. Luckily, our team came back to win the game.

On the way home, I told Judah that I was proud of him and that he played a great game. He said, "Thank You, dad." But then he said something that cut me deep to my heart. "Dad, that's why I wanted you to play catch with me, so I would be ready if the ball came to me. But I understand that you're busy. I'm not mad. I love you." I have to fight to hold back the tears every time I tell this story. I was so caught up in my work that I had forgotten about the important thing, the Main Thing - my family.

How many of us put our families on the back burner in pursuit of success? Then we try to justify our actions by saying that we are doing it for our family. Now, don't get me wrong, we all have to work and provide an income to support our family, but we should never be so focused on our careers that we neglect those who are most important to us. Will I be able to play catch with Judah every time he asks? Of course not.

The truth of the matter is that I am almost always busy doing something. But I now know that nothing is more important than my son. I now take the time to do those things that are important to him. I am deliberate about spending time with him. I don't always get it right, but I make a conscience effort not to let work consume me. And Judah notices the fact that now when he asks to spend time with me, the answer is usually yes. Whatever I'm working on can wait. It's not a life and death situation; but the relationship, or lack thereof, with our children may be. Our children are hungry for our attention, and if they don't get attention from us, they are bound to get it from someone else. And that someone else may not be a good influence. It's our responsibility.

The fact that my oldest son wants to spend time with me is a precious thing anyway. I know fathers who have teenage kids that don't want anything to do with them. They get their influences from the kids at school and the world around them. My son always wants to spend time with his "uncool" dad. I am actually very cool, but Judah doesn't think so at times.

From the time he was able to understand what a job was, he has always wanted to be like me. I was in the Marine Corps, so he said that he wanted to be a Marine. He knows all three verses of the Marine's Hymn and he sings it with vigor. I am so proud of him. I sold insurance; so of course, he wanted to sell insurance when he grew up. When I upgraded my cell phone, he asked for my old phone. It wasn't activated, so I gave it to him. When he was younger, I would often see and hear him pretending to talk to someone on the phone. When I asked who he was talking to, he would say, "I'm selling insurance dad." So I would give him pointers on how to be a good salesman. "Okay son, if they say no, that means not now. You have to follow up with them later. The fortune is in the follow-up."

So when I left the insurance industry to pursue a speaking career, it was no surprise that he said he now wants to be a professional speaker as well. And guess what? He's pretty good at it too. I've had the pleasure of hearing him speak at school (Trinitas Christian) on several occasions. Recently, he and I worked on one of his speeches together. It was some good father-son bonding time.

I was asked to be the keynote speaker at a recent Chamber event. I took Judah with me to assist. I asked him to pray for me before the event started. He also kept watch on the time as I spoke to make sure I didn't go over; and afterward, he handed out business cards to all the attendees. You should have seen him working the room. I have no doubt that you will probably meet him at one of my events offering my book. And one day, I will be at his event offering his book as well. I can't wait.

The bottom line is that I make time to include Judah in the things that I do. It would be easy for me to say, "I don't have time to play catch, read a book, attend his program, or go to his games." Remember, "If it's important to you, you will find a way; if it's not, you will find an excuse." If you struggle with "I don't have time" as I did, I have a challenge for you. For the next thirty days, instead of saying, "I don't have time," say this instead, "It's not a priority for me." They say that it takes thirty days to form a habit, either good or bad. The habit we are trying to form is making sure we focus on the Main Thing, which is our family. Think about it. How does this sound to you?

Dad, will you be at my game Saturday? I can't, son. It's not a priority for me. Mom, can you read to me? Not now, sweetie, it's not a priority for me. Dad, can you play catch with me? I wish I could, son, but it's not a priority for me.

I guarantee that you will change your tune really quickly just as I did. Life will always get in the way. We have to make time for the important things in our life. My success and my business are important to me, but they don't compare to my relationship with my children. I'm sure you would say the same thing as well. "My kids are more important than my business." But what do your actions say? Our kids grow up so quickly. Don't miss out on those precious moments for the sake of wealth. Mark 8:36 says, *"For what shall it profit a man, if he shall gain the whole world, and lose his own soul?"* A man who has the love and respect of his family is far wealthier than the man with all the gold and silver, but eventually loses his family.

If I am honest, I would have to say that I love the accolades that I receive from the audience when I finish speaking. I am showered with words of praise and adoration. It feels good to my soul and my flesh. In the past, I have given donations to charitable organizations, or held fundraisers and helped raise money for other organizations. These organizations thanked me and stated that it would not have been possible were it not for my efforts. If you were to ask anyone who knows me, I'm sure that I would receive a favorable report. I constantly have to give glory to God to keep me from being lifted up in pride. Proverbs 16:18 says, *"Pride goeth before destruction."* You may be extremely good at what you do, and everyone knows it. You may be the popular person at work, the go-to guy, the business owner, the top salesperson or even the pastor of the church. Everyone is singing your praises, except your family.

Are you one way in public and a different way at home?

The Main Thing

Does everyone respect you, except your spouse? Does everyone say that you are a man of your word, except your children? God has shown me that the only earthly opinion that should matter to me is what my wife says, what my children say, what Judah says. If you were to leave this earth tomorrow, and your family had to give your eulogy (and they had to tell the truth) what would they say? If you have to give it a second thought, I would say that it's time to start making some changes. I had to ask myself this same question, and I was not happy with the answer, so I am changing it on a daily basis. What would Judah say? Would my son have to lie at my funeral, or will he be able to speak the truth from his heart? Wow!

When I initially started working in the insurance industry, I had to take a class for my property and casualty license. The instructor had been in the industry as a salesperson for many years. During the class, the conversation led to goals. I boldly told the class that I wanted to be #1 in my region. The instructor replied, saying, "Why not #7?" I said, "#7? Are you kidding me? #7 is a loser." He said that #1 could be a loser as well.

He went on to explain that he was once #1 in his region for 3 or 4 years in a row. He and his team won every award, every trip, every bonus; and everyone knew his name. But his home life was falling apart. His kids would still be sleeping each time he went to work, and already in bed when he got home. He even worked on Saturdays. He had no time for his wife, and their marriage was falling apart. They didn't even enjoy the trips they won because their family was dysfunctional.

He was #1, and he lost his family. When he finally realized that it was not worth sacrificing his family for wealth or career, he made a change. He began taking the kids to school on the way to the office. He made sure that he was home every evening to tuck the kids into bed. He and his wife scheduled date nights. He let her know, with actions, that she was more important to him than his career was. He did a complete 180 degrees change. His marriage became better, his relationship with his kids also improved, and he eventually became a happier person as a father and husband. He gradually moved to #7 in the region, still making a very good living. His family life became so much better when he made that change that he eventually decided to stop selling altogether and simply teach insurance classes.

He taught me more that day than I've ever learned in any other insurance class or training. Being #1 in your craft or trade is perfectly fine. Just make sure that you're not sacrificing your family to do so. Ask yourself, where do I rank with my family? #1 or #7?

I decided to name this chapter "The Main Thing" after attending a Rotary meeting a few years ago. I am a member of Pensacola North Rotary, and I was visiting Suburban West Rotary this particular day. One of their members was talking about making sure that the club stayed focused on the reason they all joined Rotary. He didn't want their club to lose focus. He wanted to make sure that the members continued to do great things in the community and around the world. Rotary's slogan is Service Above Self. So he kept repeating it over and over that members should stick to The Main Thing. Let's make sure we keep The Main Thing, The Main Thing! So many times in life, we can get our priorities mixed up, turned around, and become totally unfocused; we may begin to focus on the wrong thing or less important things. Make sure you keep The Main Thing, your family, as a priority in your life. Thank you, Wayne Ethridge.

Speaking of priorities, here are the priorities that I live by - God, Family and then Business.

My desire is to have a fruitful family life along with a successful career, and that is why I put God first. Psalms 37:4 says, *"Delight yourself in the LORD; and he shall give you the desires of your heart."* None of us have the ability to make these things happen. We have to do the work; we have to do our part, but it is God who ultimately blesses us. All good gifts come from above. As business owners and sales people, we can't force anyone to purchase our product. We can only advertise, make the calls, do the presentations, study our craft, follow up, have faith, and do the work; only God can, and will, give the increase.

Matthew 6:33 says, *"Seek first the kingdom of God, and his righteousness; all these things shall be added unto you."* What are the things? They are the things that most individuals want; peace, love, health, joy, a fruitful relationship with family, and, of course, financial prosperity. The good news is that God wants these things for us as well. 3 John 1:2 says, *"Beloved, I wish above all things that thou (you) may prosper and be in health, even as thy (your) soul prospers."* God has set it up for us to win when we put Him first in our lives. Have faith and do the work (so many of us Christians miss this part).

I have tried it the other way. I tried putting business before God and family. I didn't intentionally do it, but I took my focus off of what was The Main Thing, and I almost lost my family. I convinced myself that I was doing all of this for them, and they just didn't understand. I was actually doing it for me and not them. I didn't understand that my family wanted me instead of things. It was a long road back, but once I put God first, He indeed gave me (and continues to give me) the desires of my heart. My family has a stronger bond today than ever before. No family is perfect, and from time to time we will still have minor issues. It's just life. But I tell you this: for the first time, I can honestly say there is no place else on earth that I'd rather be.

Can you honestly say that about your relationship with your spouse, children, job, and your life? Here is another challenge for you. For thirty days (same thirty days as before or a second thirty days), completely take your focus off of the "things" in life. Pray to God every day and read His word every day. Spend some "alone" time and meditate on His word. Learn what God's Word says about you and any situation that you may be facing. 1 Peter 5:7 (Amplified version) says, "*Once and for all, casting all your cares, all your worries and all your anxieties on him, for he (God) cares for you.*" Do this and you will experience peace and strength never felt before. I guarantee it. I apologize…GOD guarantees it!

I want to thank you for taking the time to read my book. I trust that you received, at least, one thing, one new idea or one revelation that you can implement in order to win in life and business.

I want to leave you with a song. I remember hearing this song a few times while watching a movies from the 70's. I never

"10 To Win"

really paid attention to the lyrics. One Sunday, while in church, my pastor, Anthony McMillan, read the lyrics to this popular song; and it blew us all away. When he finished, you could hear a pin drop in the sanctuary. It made us all re-think our priorities. I pray that it will do the same for you.

The song was written in 1974 by Harry Chapin. It topped the Billboard Hot 100. It's his only number one hit. It was nominated for a Grammy in 1975 and inducted into the Grammy Hall of Fame in 2011. The name of the song is "Cat's in the Cradle." Look it up. Listen carefully to the lyrics. Decide what's the Main Thing in your life. Because of copyright laws I can't print the lyrics, but here is a synopsis.

A child (son) is growing up right before his dad's eyes. He's learning to talk and walk and do all of the neat little things that kids do, but unfortunately like many of us the dad is too busy paying bills, working long hours, always on the go, and never having any time to spend with his son. Ironically, the son still admires his dad and wants to be just like him when he grows up.

The son is constantly asking, "When are you coming home dad?" Of course the dad doesn't know the answer but keeps reassuring his son that when he finally does come home, they will spend time together.

This goes on year after year until finally the son is in college and later has a family and job of his own. Now the tables are turned and the dad wants to spend time with the son, but at this point in his life, the son is too busy as well. He begins making the same promises to his dad that were made to him as a child.

Some call it karma. The Bible calls it sowing and reaping. Galatians 6:7 says, *"Do not be deceived. God is not mocked. Whatsoever a man sows, that shall he also reap."* Whatever we plant, we will harvest.

The dad finally realizes that his son's wishes have come true. He ended up being just like his dad. He put his work before his family. He lost sight of the Main Thing.

Folks, chapters one through nine mean absolutely nothing unless you get number ten right. Let's make sure that we keep The Main Thing, The Main Thing if we want to win in life and in business. If you haven't been establishing the right priorities in the past, I've got good news for you. There's still time to change.

Incidentally, you will be happy to know that The Trinitas Knights baseball team went undefeated the year I discovered the main thing in my life.

<u>Judah Wilmer - Trinitas Championship Trophy</u>

#10 If you want to Win in Life & Business, you have to establish the right priorities and keep the main thing, the main thing. God, Family and then Business.

"The key is not to prioritize your schedule, but to schedule your priorities." - Stephen Covey

"No one is busy; it's all about priorities." - Anonymous

Notes:

Conclusion

So there you have it. It's not earth-shattering or rocket science. It's just 10 simple concepts to live by, in order to have a more productive life and business.

Remember that everything starts with a dream. If you can dream it, and commit to it, then you can accomplish it.

Then get excited about your dream and work towards making it come true.

While you're working on your dream, be a positive example to others and lead by example.

Set SMART goals and slow down to make sure that you achieve your desired success.

Once you start, don't quit. Go all out to make sure that your dreams come true.

Surround yourself with people whom you can learn from that can help you get to the next level.

Make sure that you always do what's right along this journey and treat those around you with respect and dignity.

Treat others the way they would prefer to be treated, not

as you want to be treated.

Fear will always come, but never let fear stop you from doing what needs to be done. JUMP!

And as long as you keep your priorities straight, you can't help but be a success.

Thank you for taking the time to read my book. I sincerely hope that at least one of these concepts has shed some light on a particular situation that you may be dealing with now or possibly in the future.

If in reading this you felt the need to make a change, ponder this:

The distance between your Dreams & Reality.... Is called ACTION!!!

God bless you and remember, "10 to Win".

Stephen C. Wilmer

Steve Wilmer

Opportunities:

To schedule Steve Wilmer for a speaking engagement or live training event, go to www.SteveWilmer.com

Steve Speaks LLC provides Corporate, small business, and community speaking services. Specializing in motivation to help teams reach their goals.

Steve Wilmer is also a trainer and coach through the Risk Advisors Institute. For more information visit www.RiskAdvisorInstitute.com

"10 TO WIN"

THE TOP TEN WAYS TO WIN IN LIFE & BUSINESS

In Loving Memory

My Son

Reginald Lamar Wilmer

1985-2004

Made in the USA
Charleston, SC
23 March 2016